MW01609584

Copyright 2026 Shield of Faith Press

All rights reserved

ISBN: 978-1-967697-01-4

Direct inquiries to:

Shield of Faith Press, an AMDG Company

8399 Melrose Drive

Overland Park, KS 66214

The United States of America

Catechism of Timely Truths Opposed to Contemporary Errors

Translation of "*Lettre pastorale sur les problèmes de l'apostolat moderne – Catéchisme des vérités opportunes qui s'opposent aux erreurs contemporaines*" by Bp. Antônio de Castro Mayer, 1953.

Bp. Antônio de Castro Mayer

Table of Contents

About the Author

Bishop Antônio de Castro Mayer (1904-1991) was the Bishop of Campos in Brazil between 1949 and 1981.

As one of 12 children in the modest family of stonemason João Mayer (of German origin) and Francisca de Castro, the young de Castro Mayer was quickly noticed for his intellectual gifts upon entering the path to priesthood; for that reason he was sent to study at the Pontifical Gregorian University in Rome, where he obtained a doctorate in theology in 1928, soon after his ordination to priesthood on October 30, 1927. For the next 13 years, he taught philosophy and dogmatic theology at the major seminary of São Paulo. He then took on more responsibilities in the archdiocese of São Paulo and was appointed Coadjutor Bishop of Campos in 1948. Upon the death of the previous bishop, he became Bishop of Campos on January 3, 1949.

In performing his episcopal duties, Bp. de Castro Mayer always showed a strong attachment to the magisterium of the Church and the teachings of sacred theology. Owing to his formation as a doctor in theology, his character and ministry was more markedly "doctrinal" than that of other bishops.

Being one of the leaders of the *Coetus Internationalis Patrum* during Vatican II, together with Bp. Geraldo de Proença Sigaud and Abp. Marcel Lefebvre, he then notoriously opposed the liturgical reforms and his diocese had remained, for the whole duration of his mandate, entirely free of the new liturgy and exclusively performing the Traditional Latin Mass. He was convinced that the "New Mass" was favoring heresy, and therefore had to be avoided and opposed.

On June 30, 1988, he took part in the Écône consecrations as co-consecrator with Abp. Marcel Lefebvre. On this day, Bp. de Castro Mayer explained this radical decision (consecrating bishops without the required papal mandate) as being justified by the formal vacancy of the Holy See. He declared during a sermon: "The world may say: this consecration is being done without the visible Head of the Church. But where is the visible Head of the Church? Can we accept as the visible Head of the Church a bishop who places Pagan deities on the same level as the divinity of Our Lord Jesus Christ? [referring to the 1986 interreligious meeting in Assisi] That is not possible."[1] Witnesses have said that he declared more explicitly, after the ceremony, "There is no Pope."

We remember Bp. de Castro Mayer as one of the very few members of the pre-Vatican II ecclesiastical hierarchy who stood up for the defense of the beliefs always held by the Church, and always true in spite of the deviations of modern men.

---

1 Quoted in the review *Sodalitium*, issue 54, p. 38.

Preface

We are glad to present the English translation, drawn from the French version, of the *Pastoral Letter on the Problems of the Modern Apostolate* and the *Catechism of Timely Truths Opposed to Contemporary Errors* by Bishop Antonio de Castro Mayer, who was bishop of Campos, Brazil, from 1949 to 1981. Some of the notes are drawn from the 2006 edition of *Editions du Sel*.

Promulgated on January 6, 1953, it is divided into three parts. After a strongly doctrinal introduction on the problems of the modern apostolate or – to use the words of Bishop de Castro Mayer himself – on "the integrity of the faith," it contains a "Catechism of timely truths opposed to contemporary errors" and, finally, a series of directives addressed to the diocesan clergy.

The introduction (the pastoral letter) very aptly denounces the current evil, which is a loss of the spirit of faith and the sense of truth. It is an important document that should be read carefully.

The Catechism is designed according to a method of admirable clarity. For each question addressed, it first states the false or, at least, dangerous proposition for faith and morals, which is like the maxim of contemporary error. Next to it, it gives the corresponding Catholic proposition. An explanation rich in quotations from pontifical documents justifies the condemnation of the erroneous proposition and comments on the Catholic proposition.

This pastoral letter was widely distributed in Brazil and was translated and disseminated in France (ed. *Cité Catholique*, Paris, 1953), Italy (*Instituto Editoriale Bartolo Longo*, Pompeii, 1954; *Edizione del Alberto*, Turin, 1964), Spain (*Colleccion Fé Integra, dos Padres Cooperadores Paroquiais de Cristo Rei*, Madrid, 1955), Argentina (*Libreria Católica Accion*, Buenos Aires, 1959), and Canada (*La Cité Catholique*, Quebec, reprinted from *Verbe*, no. 103, 1962).

It should be noted that this Catechism was written in 1953, only nine years before the opening of the Vatican II, and sixteen years before the promulgation of the new Mass. Yet everything is there: the "active participation" of the faithful, the "priesthood of the laity," the replacement of the altar with a table, Mass facing the people, the elimination of images of saints, contempt for popular piety, etc. And the same observation applies to the other chapters of the Catechism, devoted to methods of apostolate, spiritual life, the new morality, Liberalism, the relationship between Church and State, etc. This shows us that the conciliar heresy had been brewing for a long time, waiting for its moment. The interest of Bishop de Castro Mayer's Catechism is that it goes back to the principles of the errors it denounces. In order to rebuild solidly, we must do the same: return to Catholic principles and not allow ourselves to be seduced by this global reform which would only ratify the fundamental deviations.

— The editors.

Pastoral Letter on the Problems of the Modern Apostolate

To the Most Reverend Secular and Regular Clergy. Greetings, peace, and blessings in Our Lord Jesus Christ.

Beloved and zealous sons and cooperators,

Of all the duties incumbent upon the bishop, none surpasses in importance that of providing the sheep entrusted to him by the Holy Ghost with the salutary nourishment of revealed truth.

This obligation is particularly urgent in our day. For the immense crisis in which the world is struggling is ultimately the result of the fact that the thoughts and actions of men have been dissociated from the teachings and norms laid down by the Church; and only a return of humanity to the true faith can remedy this crisis.

It is indeed of the utmost importance to launch, in a united and disciplined manner, the Catholic forces, the entire peaceful army of Christ the King, to conquer the peoples who moan in the shadows of death, deluded by heresy or schism, by the superstitions of ancient Paganism or by the many idols of modern Neo-Paganism.

In order for this general offensive, so desired by the supreme pontiffs, to be effective and victorious, it is necessary that Catholic forces themselves remain pure from the errors they must combat. The preservation of the faith among the sons of the Church is therefore a necessary and sovereign measure for the enthronement of Christ's reign on earth.

The Evolution Of Heresies And The Trap Of Semi-Heresies

History teaches us that the temptation against the faith, always the same in its essential elements, presents itself in a new guise in every age. Arianism, for example, which exerted such a powerful force of seduction in the fourth century, would have been of little interest to the frivolous, Voltairean Europeans of the eighteenth century; and the declared and radical Atheism of the nineteenth century would have had little chance of success in the time of Wycliffe and John Huss.

Moreover, temptation against faith tends to act with different intensity in each generation. It manages to lead one generation completely into heresy. In another, without formally and openly tearing it away from the maternal bosom of the Church, it instills its spirit, so that many Catholics who correctly recite the formulas of faith and believe, sometimes sincerely, that they adhere without restriction to the teachings of the Church's magisterium, their hearts beat under the influence of doctrines condemned by the Church.

This is a common experience. How often do we see Catholics around us who are proud of being children of the Church and never miss an opportunity to proclaim their faith, yet at the same time, in their way of looking at ideas, customs, events, and everything that the press, cinema, radio, or television broadcast daily, are in no way different from skeptics, agnostics, or the indifferent! They recite the Creed correctly and, at prayer time, show themselves to be irreproachable Catholics, but the spirit that, consciously or unconsciously, animates them in all circumstances of life is Agnostic, Naturalistic, Liberal.

As we can see, these are souls divided by conflicting tendencies. On the one hand, they feel the seduction of the spirit of the age. On the other hand, perhaps through family heritage, they still retain something of the pure, immutable, and unquenchable brilliance of Catholic doctrine. And, since any state of inner division is unnatural to man, these souls try to restore unity and peace within themselves by amalgamating into a single body of doctrine the errors they admire and the truths they do not want to break with.

This tendency to reconcile irreconcilable extremes, to find a middle ground between truth and error, has manifested itself since the origins of the Church. Already, the divine Savior had warned his apostles: "No man can serve two masters" (Mt 6:24). When Arianism was condemned, this tendency gave rise to Semi-Arianism. When Pelagianism was condemned, it gave rise to Semi-Pelagianism. Protestantism having been struck down at the Council of Trent, it gave rise to Jansenism. It also gave birth to Modernism, condemned by St. Pius X, a monstrous confluence of Atheism, Rationalism, Evolutionism, Pantheism, a school of apostasy determined to treacherously stab the Church in the back. The Modernist sect's goal was to remain within the Church while distorting, through sophistry, insinuations, and reservations, the true doctrine that it outwardly pretended to accept.

This tendency has by no means ceased; one might even say that it is part of the history of the Church. This is what we can deduct from the words of the gloriously reigning Supreme Pontiff [Pius XII] in his address to the Lenten preachers in Rome in 1944:

"A fact that is always repeated in the history of the Church is that when Christian faith and morals are opposed by strong contrary currents of error or vicious appetites, attempts arise to overcome the difficulties by means of some convenient compromise, or to evade them, or even to close one's eyes to them " (AAS 36, page 73).

Is Doctrinal Formation A Waste Of Time?

If you warn your parishioners against Spiritism, Protestantism, or Atheism, dear sons and beloved cooperators, no one will be surprised. But in this Pastoral Letter, we urge you to denounce opinions which, even among Catholics themselves, very often corrupt the integrity of the faith. Will you be well understood on this point as well?

It may seem to many, even among the most pious, that you are wasting your time, for it will be difficult for them to understand why you are exhausting yourselves to perfect the faith that some already possess, however poorly, when it would be better to seek to convert those who are outside the Church and await your apostolate. It will seem to them that you are showering superfluous treasures on those who are already rich, while leaving those who are starving without bread.

Others will think you are imprudent, because, since professing to be Catholic is already so meritorious in such a hostile century, you run the risk of losing even the best if you are not content with this or that adherence to the general lines of the faith, without overburdening the faithful with irritating minutiae.

It is of the utmost importance, beloved sons and dear cooperators, that you first enlighten your parishioners on these two objections. Otherwise, your action will be ineffective and, because of the unfortunate times in which we live, your zeal will be misunderstood. There will be no shortage of people who will see in this not a natural movement of the Church, which, through its best workers and models, rejects, as a living organism, any foreign body, but, on the contrary, the unintelligent and obstinate action of exalted champions.

Therefore, above all, show that, by its very nature, faith is not satisfied with what some call its general outlines, but demands integrity and completeness.

To make yourself understood, give the example of the virtue of chastity. In this regard, any compromise takes on the character of a dark stain, and any imprudence puts it entirely at risk. The pure soul has been compared to a person standing on a sphere; as long as it maintains its position of balance, it has nothing to fear; but the slightest imprudence on its part will cause it to roll into the abyss. This is why moralists and spiritual authors are unanimous in affirming that the essential condition for maintaining angelic virtue consists in vigilant and uncompromising prudence.

The same can rightly be said of faith. As long as Catholics maintain perfect equilibrium, their perseverance will be assured and easy. This point of balance, however, does not consist in an approximate acceptance of the faith in its general outlines; it is the clear and total profession of the doctrine of the Church, a proclamation made not with the lips, but with the whole soul. This profession of the Catholic implies the loyal and consistent acceptance not only of what the Magisterium teaches, but also of all the logical consequences of that teaching. It is necessary, in fact, that the faithful possess that living faith by which they can submit their personal reason to the infallible Magisterium and discern with insight everything that directly or indirectly opposes the teaching of the Church. But if they were to abandon this position of perfect balance, even slightly, they would begin to feel the pull of the abyss. That is why, moved by prudence and in the interest of the flock entrusted to us, we address this pastoral letter on the integrity of the faith to you, our beloved children.

The Spirit Of Faith Is Necessary For All

In this regard, it is necessary to insist once again on a point of Church doctrine that is often forgotten. Let no one think that such an enlightened and robust faith is the privilege of scholars, so that only they can be recommended to the ideal position of balance described above. Faith is a virtue, and in the Holy Church, virtues are accessible to all the faithful, whether ignorant or learned, rich or poor, teachers or disciples. Christian hagiography proves this. Saint Joan of Arc, an uneducated shepherdess from the village of

Domrémy, confounded her judges with the sagacity with which she responded to the theological sophistry they used to lead her into erroneous propositions and thus justify her condemnation to death. Saint Clement Mary Hofbauer, in the 19th century, a humble manual laborer who attended theology classes at the illustrious University of Vienna out of personal interest, discerned in one of his teachers the evil influence of Jansenism, which escaped the discernment of all his students and other professors. "I confess to thee, O Father, Lord of heaven and earth, because thou hast hidden these things from the wise and prudent, and hast revealed them to little ones." (Luke 10:21). In order for us to have a people who are firm and logical in their faith, it is not necessary for us to make them a people of theologians. It is enough that those who deeply love the Church learn the revealed truths according to their level of general culture and possess the virtues of purity and humility necessary to truly believe, understand, and enjoy the things of God. Similarly, in order to have a truly pure people, it is not necessary to make every believer a moralist. Fundamental principles, and basic knowledge of everyday life, dictated in large part by a well-formed Christian conscience, are sufficient. Thus, we very often see ignorant people who have superior judgment, prudence, and elevation of soul to those of many learned moralists.

What we have just said about the perseverance of an individual also applies to the perseverance of peoples. When the population of a diocese possesses the integrity of the Catholic spirit, it is able, with the help of God's grace, to withstand the assaults of impiety. But when no one possesses it, when even those usually considered pious do not love and seek this integrity, what are we to think of such a population?

Without The Spirit Of Faith, Faith Is In Danger

Reading history, it is difficult to understand how certain

peoples, endowed with a numerous and enlightened hierarchy, an educated and influential clergy, and illustrious and wealthy educational and charitable institutions, such as Sweden, Norway, and Denmark in the 16th century, could slip, from one moment to the next, from the complete and peaceful profession of the Catholic faith to open and formal heresy, almost without resistance and, to tell the truth, almost imperceptibly. What is the reason for such a great disaster? When the faith began to decline in these countries, it was already nothing more than external formulas, repeated without love or conviction, in most people's minds. Thus, a simple royal whim was enough to cut down the dense, centuries-old tree. The sap had long since ceased to flow in the leaves or the trunk. The spirit of faith no longer existed in these regions.

This is what Blessed Pius X[1] understood with angelic lucidity in his vigorous struggle against Modernism. A most merciful pastor, he illuminated the Church of God with the sweet radiance of his heavenly gentleness. However, he did not fear to denounce the authors of the Modernist error within the Church itself and to point them out to the execration of the good with these vehement words: "He will not stray from the truth who considers them [the Modernists] as the most dangerous enemies of the Church."[2]

We can judge how painful it was for the very gentle pontiff to use so much energy. But his contemporaries did not fail to recognize the outstanding service he was thus rendering to the Church. In this regard, the great Cardinal Mercier affirmed that if, at the time of Luther and Calvin, the Church had had popes of the caliber of Pius X, it is doubtful that Protestant heresy would have succeeded in detaching a third of Europe from the true Church.[3] For all these reasons, beloved co-

1 [TN] Saint Pius X was beatified on June 3, 1951, and canonized on May 29, 1954. The Pastoral Letter and Catechism were issued in 1953.
2 Encyclical *Pascendi*.
3 See Cardinal Merry del Val, *Souvenirs of Pope Pius X*, Madrid, Atenas, 1946, p. 51.

workers, see how important it is to watch with the greatest zeal to keep the sons of the Holy Church in the fullness of faith and the spirit of faith.

The Doctrinal Formation Of Christians Even Serves The Infidels

Show also how mistaken are those who suppose that the time and effort spent on perfecting the faithful in the faith are, so to speak, stolen from the infidels. Above all, by your example and your words, you can prove that these two attitudes are in no way incompatible: *Oportet hæc facere et illa non omittere* [This must be done and that must not be omitted]. Moreover, the integrity of the faith produces so many fruits of virtue among Catholics and spreads so vividly throughout the Church the good odor of Jesus Christ that it effectively attracts the infidels to herself, so that the good done to the children of the Church will necessarily benefit those who are outside the fold. Finally, one of the fruits of fervent faith will necessarily be apostolic zeal. What is multiplying apostles if not doing good to unbelievers?

Therefore, we cannot accept this dissociation between the time devoted to the faithful and that devoted to non-believers, as if our divine Savior, in forming his apostles and disciples, had perfected a group of privileged individuals and lost interest in the salvation of the rest of humanity!

Can One Be Too Traditional?

May the shining example of the Vicar of Christ [Pius XII] , encourage you to do so! No pope, no doubt, has had to face so many powerful enemies outside the Church. However, he did not neglect the "errors that creep among the faithful"[4] and warned us against them in a series of documents, such as the encyclical Mediator Dei, the Apostolic Constitution

4 *Mystici Corporis*, AAS 35, p. 197.

Bis sæculari die, the encyclical *Humani generis* and, more recently, the address to religious sisters (September 15, 1952), in which he holds certain Catholic writers, both clerical and lay, who distort Catholic doctrine regarding the preeminence of celibacy over the married state, largely responsible for the decline in vocations. And more particularly, with regard to Brazil, the zeal of the Holy See in the face of the internal problems of the Church is clearly evident in the Letter of the Sacred Congregation of Seminaries and Universities, which we strongly recommend you read carefully.[5]

In striving to maintain the traditional spirit of the Holy Church among the faithful, you must ensure that it is not in any way deviated from its authentic meaning. In this Pastoral Letter, we consider, taken to the extreme, the spirit of conciliation with the errors of our time. However, this bad tendency can be opposed by a symmetrical error. It is important to show what it is.

There is no reason to fear excess in the traditional spirit. For this spirit is one of the essential elements of the Catholic mentality, of what is rightly called the Catholic sense. Now, the Catholic sense constitutes, in itself, the very excellence of the virtue of faith. To fear that someone possesses too much Catholic sense would be tantamount to fearing that they have too much faith! It is important to avoid misunderstanding this spirit of faith, which results more in an attachment to outward form, to pure appearance, to simple ritual, rather than an adherence to the spirit that animates and explains form, appearance, and ritual. Exaggerations of this nature are possible; however, in your duty of vigilance, they do not deserve as much attention as the abusive propensity for novelty and the systematic aversion to tradition. This is what the Sacred Congregation for Seminaries wisely sought to convey in its Letter to the Brazilian Episcopate: "The most urgent danger today is not that of an overly rigid and exclusive attachment to Tradition, but mainly that of

---

5 See AAS 42, p. 836 ff.

an excessive and imprudent taste for all the novelties that appear, whatever they may be" (AAS 42, page 837). And the Sacred Congregation adds with foresight: "It is certainly to the snobbery of novelties that we owe the proliferation of errors, hidden under an appearance of truth and, more often than not, under pretentious and obscure terminology" (*ibid.*, page 939).

An example of a misunderstanding of the spirit of tradition can be seen in the archaism referred to by the Holy Father Pius XII in the encyclical *Mediator Dei*. Out of an excessive attachment to ancient rites and forms, simply because they are ancient, some liturgists claim to be restoring the table-shaped altar and other practices of the early Church.[6] As if, throughout history, the spirit of the Church had not been able to express itself little by little, through new forms and new rites, according to the diversity of times and places.

Extremes meet, and the most opposing excesses easily unite against the truth. The danger of this misunderstood traditional spirit is most often encountered among the very proponents of novelty, such as Luther, Jansenius, the promoters of the false council of Pistoia, and, in our century, the Modernists.

Natural Cause Of Heresy: Fallen Nature

Explain clearly to the faithful under your care, dear cooperators, the origin of these errors. On the one hand, they arise from the weakness of fallen human nature. Sensuality and pride have always provoked, and will continue to provoke until the end of time, the rebellion of certain sons of the Church against the doctrine and spirit of Our Lord Jesus Christ. Already St. Paul warned the early Christians that there would arise among them "men speaking perverse things, to draw away disciples after them" (Acts 20:30); "vain talkers and seducers" (Titus 1:10) "evil men and seducers [that] shall grow worse and worse: erring, and driving into error" (2

6 See AAS 39, p. 545.

Timothy 3:13).

Some seem to think that, in recent centuries, the progress of the Church has been such that we no longer need to fear the emergence of crises caused by pride and lust within her. However, to cite only very recent examples, Blessed Pius X declared in his encyclical *Pascendi* that the instigators of rebellion, such as those we are discussing, were not only frequent in his time, but would become more frequent as we approached the end of time. And indeed, in the encyclical *Humani generis*, the Holy Father Pius XII complains that "there is no shortage today those who, as in apostolic times, love novelty more than is lawful and also fear being considered ignorant of the progress of science, try to escape the guidance of the sacred magisterium and, for this reason, find themselves in danger of gradually straying from revealed truth and leading others with them into error" (AAS42, page 564).

Preternatural Cause Of Heresy: The Action Of The Devil. The Fifth Column

Such is the natural genesis of the errors and crises with which we are concerned. However, it is necessary to consider not only the deficiencies of fallen nature, but also the action of the devil. The latter has been given, until the end of time, the power to tempt men in all virtues and, consequently, also in the virtue of faith, which is the very foundation of supernatural life. It is therefore evident that, until the end of time, the Church will be exposed to internal outbreaks of the spirit of heresy and that there is no progress that can, so to speak, definitively immunize her against this evil. There is no need to demonstrate that the devil strives to produce such crises. The allies he manages to implant within the faithful armies are his most precious instrument of combat. Current experience shows that a fifth column surpasses even the most terrible weapons in effectiveness. With the revolutionary tumor forming in Catholic circles, forces are divided, and energies that should be used entirely in the fight against the external enemy are exhausted in discussions between brothers. And if, to avoid such discussions, the good people put an end to the strife, even greater is the triumph of hell, which can plant its banner within the very city of God and rapidly and easily expand its conquests.

If at some point hell ceased to attempt such a lucrative maneuver, one could say that during that time the devil would have ceased to exist.

Such is the dual origin, natural and supernatural, of the internal crises of the Church.

Heresy Progresses In Disguise

As you can see, these two causes are perpetual, and their effect will also be perpetual. In other words, the Church will always have to suffer from the internal irruption of the spirit of darkness.

To shed light on what your mission should be, it is important to recall the tactics it adopts. In order to keep its actions clandestine, it is important for it to disguise them. Concealment is the fundamental rule of those who act secretly in the camp of the adversary. To achieve his ends, the devil instills a spirit of confusion that seduces souls, leading them to profess error cleverly concealed under the appearance of truth. In this struggle, do not expect the adversary to issue judgments that are openly contrary to already established truths. He will only do so when he considers himself to be completely in control of the field. More often than not, he will cause "errors to proliferate, hidden under the appearance of truth [...] with pretentious and obscure terminology."[7] And the manner in which this proliferation of errors is propagated will itself be masked and insidious. The Holy Father Pius XII describes the process as follows: "Those who, either out of

7 Letter from the Sacred Congregation of Seminaries to the bishops of Brazil; AAS 42, p. 839.

a reprehensible desire for innovation or for some laudable motive, propagate these new opinions, do not always propose them with the same intensity, nor with the same clarity, nor in identical terms, nor always with apparent unanimity; what some teach today secretly, with certain precautions and distinctions, others, more daring, will spread tomorrow openly and without restraint, to the scandal of the great many, especially the young clergy, and to the detriment of ecclesiastical authority. It is their habit to treat these subjects more cautiously in books that are published; then to speak more freely about them in pamphlets distributed under the cloak and in conferences or meetings. And these doctrines are spread not only among members of both clergy, in seminaries and religious institutes, but also among lay people, mainly those who devote themselves to teaching young people."[8]

Thus you should not be surprised if sometimes only a few of you discern the error in propositions that to many will seem clear and orthodox, or at least confusing but open to a good interpretation; or if you find yourselves in certain environments where half-truths are cleverly arranged to spread error in such a way that it is difficult to combat.[9] The opponent's tactic has been precisely calculated to put those who oppose him in this embarrassing position. In this way, he will sometimes arouse antipathy against you, even from people who have no intention of promoting evil. They will label you visionaries, fanatics, or even slanderers. Is this not precisely what the stubborn glorifiers of the *Sillon* and Marc Sangnier said in France against Blessed Pius X? Out of fear of such criticism, will you retreat before the adversary and leave the gates of the city of God open?

It is certain that you must carefully avoid, in the eyes of God, any excess, any hastiness, any unfounded judgment. But you must also cry out whenever the adversary, disguised

8 Encyclical *Humani generis*; AAS 42, p. 565.
9 [TN] We can't help but notice how closely this description of the methods of heresy corresponds to what was achieved by the Progressive faction at the Second Vatican Council.

in sheep's clothing, appears before you, without yielding an inch of ground for fear that he will accuse you of excesses that your conscience does not reproach you for.

By doing so, you will be obeying the express intentions of the Holy Father. In all the documents he has published on this subject, the gloriously reigning sovereign pontiff recommends to bishops and priests throughout the world that they diligently instruct the faithful, so that they may not be misled by the veiled errors circulating among them.

The Importance Of Prevention: Today, Everyone Is Threatened

The doctrinal teaching advocated by the Holy Father must be both preventive and repressive. Priests whose parishes do not appear to have been affected by error should not consider themselves exempt from taking action. Given the guise under which these errors are cloaked, and given the sometimes almost imperceptible methods used by their proponents to spread them, few priests can be certain that all their sheep are safe.

Moreover, the good shepherd is not content with remedying evil: he has a grave duty to ward it off. Let us not be like the man in the Gospel who slept while his enemy sowed weeds among his wheat. The simple obligation to prevent will justify the efforts you undertake in this direction.

The errors we are concerned with may be more intense in one country and less so in another. However, their spread throughout the Catholic world is already widespread enough for the Holy Father to draw attention to them in documents addressed not to any particular nation, but to the bishops of the whole world.

For we live today in a world without borders, in which thoughts spread rapidly through the press, and especially through radio, to the ends of the earth. A false proposition made, for example, in Paris, can be heard and received on the same day in faraway places such as Australia, India, or Brazil. And if there is still some small place where extreme ignorance or excessive backwardness creates an obstacle to the penetration of true or false ideas, no one could include in this category the populous centers of our beloved diocese, at the head of which is our episcopal city, renowned throughout Brazil for the cultural value of its sons and the capital influence it has always been honored to exert on the national political scene.

Schematic Form Of This Catechism

We say a word on the method we are adopting. Given that, in its Letter to the Brazilian bishops, the Sacred Congregation of Seminaries spoke of a "proliferation of errors," and that these are indeed very numerous, it would be excessively long to explain and censure the main ones in a discursive form. We prefer a schematic form. That is why we have developed a short Catechism of the truths most currently under threat, each accompanied by the error that opposes it and a brief commentary. For the sake of convenience, we have preceded the true statement with the false or dangerous one. But your effort to denounce error should lead each believer to an accurate knowledge of the true teaching of the Church. Only in this way will we have done positive and lasting work.

The Purpose Of This Catechism: To Learn How To Counter Seemingly Harmless Formulas

Finally, a comment on the way in which false or dangerous statements are presented in the Catechism. We have tried to express them as faithfully as possible, without removing their appearance or even the fragments of truth they contain. Only in this way will the Catechism be useful, for only in this way will it reveal the expressions under which error usually hides, and the appearances with which it tries to attract the sympathy of good people. For the most important thing in this matter is not to prove that a particular phrase is wrong, but that a particular false doctrine is actually contained in a particular formula that appears harmless and even sympathetic.

That is why we have also repeated several more or less equivalent formulas. The aim is to draw your attention to the various formulations in which the same error can creep in.

We have not only included doctrinal theses in the propositions. You will also find formulated in propositions ways of acting that flow directly from false doctrine.

As you will easily see, we have taken care to follow the Apostle's advice: "prove all things; hold fast that which is good" (1 Thessalonians 5:21). Therefore, in our refutations, we have sought to show in its entirety the grain of truth contained in the tendencies we are combating. For the Church is a patient and prudent mother who condemns with caution and considers as her heritage every truth wherever it is found.

This point must be emphasized. The truths recalled here are not the heritage or property of any person, group, or school of thought. Orthodoxy is the Church's own treasure, in which everyone must share and over which no one has a monopoly. That is why, beloved cooperators, when you disseminate the teachings found here, always present them for what they really are: the total and exclusive fruit of the wisdom of the Holy Church.

It is not difficult to see that these errors, generally speaking, in terms that strive to appear correct, are the doctrines that exert the greatest influence in today's world and constitute the typical features of today's Neo-Paganism: pantheistic Evolutionism, Naturalism, Secularism, absolute Egalitarianism, which rises up in the political and social sphere against all legitimate supremacy and which, in the religious sphere, tends to suppress the distinction instituted by Jesus Christ between hierarchy and faithful people, clergy and laity.

These, beloved and dear cooperators, are the proposals to which we wish to draw your attention.

For the greatest success of your action, we have accompanied them with practical guidelines that you will find in the second part of this Letter.

Recommended Reading

In our Pastoral Letter, it is clear that we have not presumed to set forth the entire Catholic doctrine on the subject, but only some of the most pertinent observations. Your diligence, dear sons, will supplement, from the sources available to you, what we have not been able to set forth here. We particularly recommend the reading of the encyclicals *Pascendi, Mystici Corporis Christi, Mediator Dei, Humani generis,* the Apostolic Letter *Notre charge apostolique,* the Apostolic Constitution *Bis sæculari die,* the Exhortation to the Clergy *Menti nostra,* and the Papal Addresses and Radio Messages, especially the Radio Messages on Christmas Eve, the Radio Message of March 23, 1952, on the new morality (AAS 44, page 270 ff.), the radio message to the *Katholikentag* in Vienna (September 14, 1952), the addresses to the Catholic Association of Italian Workers (AAS 40, page 331 ff.), to the delegates of the International Congress of Social Studies, meeting in Rome in 1950 (AAS 42, page 451 ff.), to the members of the ninth congress of the International Union of Catholic Employers' Associations (AAS 41, page 283 ff.), to the members of the international congress of the Universal Movement for a World Confederation (AAS 43, page 278), to Italian Catholic Action and to Marian Congregations in April 1951 (AAS 43, page 375), on the occasion of the closing of the International Congress of the Lay Apostolate (AAS 43, page 784 ff.), to the Association of French Fathers (AAS 43, page 730 ff.), to the participants in the congress of the Italian Catholic Union of Midwives (AAS 43, page 835 ff.), and to the superiors general of religious orders and congregations. We also recommend the Letter from the Congregation for Seminaries to the Brazilian episcopate (AAS 42, page 836 ff.), a clear and balanced document that addresses this issue as it pertains to Brazil.

The words of the Holy Father are always beneficial and effective in uplifting the soul and guiding it towards a moral and spiritual life. Let us make good use of the documents mentioned above,[10] for they settle many social, political, and moral issues that have been obscured, especially since the last war.

***

---

10 [TN] It should be noted that most of these documents were published in *Catolicismo*, the diocesan bulletin of Dom Antonio de Castro Mayer. He read them in the original text, i.e., in Latin, in the *Acta Apostolicæ Sedis* (AAS), references to which are scattered throughout his pastoral letters.

Catechism of Timely Truths
Opposed to Contemporary Errors

I — On the Liturgy

— 1 —

When the faithful attend Holy Mass and pronounce the words of consecration with the celebrant, they cooperate in the transubstantiation and sacrifice.
The faithful are unable to "concelebrate" with the priest and cooperate in transubstantiation because they have not received the sacrament of Holy Orders, which confers this power.

Explanation

Only the sacrament of Holy Orders confers the power and capacity to effect transubstantiation in the sacrifice of the New Law. The ordinary faithful are therefore incapable of doing so.

This proposition renews the Protestant heresy condemned by the Council of Trent (sess. 23, cap. 4) and again proscribed by *Mediator Dei* [November 20, 1947] of His Holiness Pius XII (*Acta Apostolicae Sedis*, year and volume 39, page 556; *Pontifical Documents* of Solesmes, *The Liturgy*, no. 570).

— 2 —

The faithful "concelebrate" the holy sacrifice of the Mass with the priest.
The faithful participate in the sacrifice of the Mass.

Explanation

28   CATECHISM OF TIMELY TRUTHS

These two statements require a brief explanation. It can never be said that the faithful "concelebrate" with the priest, because the term "concelebrate" refers, in the Church, to Masses where there are several celebrants. All then actively contribute to the offering of the sacrifice and to transubstantiation. This is the case, for example, in priestly ordination Masses, in which the new priests concelebrate Mass with the bishop.

Similarly, the statement that the faithful participate in the sacrifice of the Mass requires explanation. Many understand it to mean that the faithful "concelebrate" the sacrifice. This would be a repetition of the error discussed in § 1. Others understand it as if the priest were merely a representative of the people, whose priestly acts would have value only insofar as he represents the people. This is not how it should be understood, according to the teaching of *Mediator Dei*.[11]

In reality, the priest is not a delegate of the people,[12] because he is chosen by divine vocation and engendered by the sacrament of Holy Orders.[13] This does not mean that the priest, in a certain sense, does not represent the people. He represents them insofar as he represents Jesus Christ, head of the Mystical Body, of which the faithful are members[14] and, when the priest offers at the altar, he does so in the name of Christ, the principal priest, who offers on behalf of all the members of his Mystical Body. Thus, in a certain sense, the sacrifice is offered in the name of the people. That is why the people must participate in the sacrifice. How? *Mediator Dei* says: "If the people offer at the same time as the priest, [... it is] because they unite their vows of praise, impetration, expiation, and thanksgiving to the vows or mental intentions of the priest, and even of the High Priest, in order to present them to God the Father in the very external rite of the priest offering the victim."[15]

11 AS 39, pp. 555-556.
12 *Mediator Dei*, AAS 39, p. 538.
13 *Mediator Dei*, ibid., p. 539.
14 *Mediator Dei*, ibid., p. 538.
15 id., p. 556.

There is therefore a real meaning to the expression "participate," which can be used if care is taken to exclude any other less accurate meanings.

— 3 —

The faithful who follow the Mass in their missal participate in the Mass; the faithful who follow the Mass in any other way merely attend it.

The participation of the faithful in the holy sacrifice of the Mass consists in union with the intentions of the High Priest, Jesus Christ, and of the celebrating priest. Any method (missal, rosary, meditation) that effectively brings about this union is perfect.

Explanation

The refuted maxim renews the Jansenist spirit contained in Quesnel's proposition, condemned by Clement XI in the Bull *Unigenitus* of September 8, 1713: "To snatch from the simple people this consolation of joining their voice to the voice of the whole Church is a custom contrary to the apostolic practice and to the intention of God." (prop. 86, DS 2486).

In itself, this is a consequence of the erroneous doctrine that the faithful "concelebrate" Holy Mass with the priest: they must therefore recite the liturgical words with him. Those who do not recite these words do not "participate" in Mass, but merely "attend" it in a purely "passive" manner. *Mediator Dei*, on the contrary, insists on union with the intentions of Jesus Christ and the celebrant, and gives the faithful complete freedom as to the method to be used to achieve this goal. However, we are far from discouraging the practice of paying attention to everything that is said at Mass, reading one's missal, and following the prayers and ceremonies of the Holy Sacrifice, etc.

Just as we must avoid the confusion — characteristic of the reformers of the 16th century — between the faithful and the priest, so too must we respect the freedom of the Holy Ghost who, given the obedience that the faithful owe to the Holy Church, guides them by his graces according to his ineffable good pleasure: "*Spiritus ubi vult spirat* — The Spirit breatheth where he will" (John 3:8).

— 4 —

One should attend Mass only by following the words of the missal. Private prayers such as the rosary, meditation, etc. should be excluded during the sacrifice. Only the dialogued Mass and the "*versus populum*" [facing the people] Mass are in harmony with the condition of the faithful during the holy sacrifice.

The use of the missal, the recitation of the rosary, meditation, and other appropriate prayers are all excellent ways to attend the holy sacrifice of the Mass. The faithful are therefore free to choose what best contributes to their union with the intentions of Jesus Christ and the priest who celebrates. All methods of attending Mass approved by the Holy Church are in harmony with the condition of the faithful during the Holy Sacrifice. Any exclusivity on this point is reprehensible.

Explanation

The refuted proposition is closely linked to the false principles of the formal priesthood of the faithful, as we have shown above.

The encyclical *Mediator Dei* approves and supports the true liturgical movement. Anything that leads the faithful to know and love the sacred liturgy deserves praise. The evil begins when false theological interpretations corrupt the spirit in which liturgical piety is propagated. It is on this observation that *Mediator Dei* bases its censure and condemnation of the extravagances that arise in the realm of liturgical piety.

– 5 –

The altar must be shaped like a table to recall the Eucharistic Supper.

"One would be straying from the straight path were he to wish the altar restored to its primitive tableform" (*Mediator Dei*).

Explanation

It is important to emphasize the doctrinal consistency that exists between the various propositions refuted thus far. They proceed from the false assumption that the faithful participate in the priesthood of Jesus Christ in the same way as priests, although perhaps to a lesser degree. However, there is a specific difference between these two participations, which the Holy Father [Pius XII] does not hesitate to compare to the difference between a pagan and a believer. Just as the pagan is separated from union with the Mystical Body of Christ and is therefore incapable of any act proper to that body, so the simple faithful are excluded from the priesthood proper to priests and are radically incapable of performing any specifically priestly act (see *Mediator Dei*, AAS 39, page 539). The error refuted is a Protestant novelty that the Jansenists, driven by the same spirit of internal reform, sought to introduce into the Church so that it might be transformed from a monarchical and aristocratic society into a democratic one.

Let us pay attention to this proposition of the Synod of Pistoia, condemned by Pius VI's bull *Auctorem fidei* (August 28, 1794): "The proposition which states 'that power has been given by God to the Church, that it might be communicated to the pastors who are its ministers for the salvation of souls,' if thus understood that the power of ecclesiastical ministry and of rule is derived from the community of the faithful to the pastors, is heretical." (prop. 2, DS 2602).

– 6 –

Communion outside Mass, visits to the Blessed Sacrament, worship of the Holy Species, perpetual adoration, and the blessing of the Blessed Sacrament are forms of extra-liturgical piety and, as such, should be gradually eliminated.

All forms of worship of the Blessed Sacrament are precious forms of piety and, as such, should be encouraged. Although *intra missam* [during Mass] communion should be encouraged, receiving Holy Communion outside of Mass is a regular means of participating in the Eucharistic sacrifice (cf. *Mediator Dei*).

Explanation

The refuted maxim presupposes that all forms of private piety are superfluous, which is an error condemned by *Mediator Dei* (AAS 39, pages 565-566 and 583). It also renews the spirit of the propositions condemned by the Council of Trent in canons 5, 6, and 7 of session XIII (S 1655-1657).

– 7 –

The simultaneous celebration of several Masses breaks the unity of the communal sacrifice.

The simultaneity of several Masses does not break the unity of the Church's communal sacrifice.

Explanation

"Some even assert that priests cannot offer the divine host on several altars at the same time, because by doing so they divide the community and jeopardize its unity." This idea is rejected by *Mediator Dei*. The reason is obvious: the sacrifice of the Mass has value only through its intrinsic relationship with the sacrifice of the cross, which was unique and valid for all time. So that, even if there are several Masses, the essential unity of the sacrifice remains. The refuted maxim recalls the Jansenist error condemned by Pius VI's Bull *Auctorem fidei* on

August 28, 1794, no. 31, where it is stated: "The proposition of the synod enunciating that it is fitting, in accordance with the order of divine services and ancient custom that there be only one altar in each temple, and therefore, that it is pleased to restore that custom, is rash, injurious to the very ancient pious custom flourishing and approved for these many centuries in the Church, especially in the Latin Church." (DS 2631).

— 8 —

There should be no other image on the altars than that of the crucifix.
There is no objection whatsoever to there being images other than the crucifix on altars, provided that they do not occupy the place reserved for the latter.

Explanation

The custom of placing images on the altar is in full accordance with Catholic doctrine concerning the worship due to them.

The refuted proposition is contrary to the spirit advised by *Mediator Dei*, which recommends the display of images of saints in churches for the edification of the faithful and reproves those who would remove these images (AAS 39, pages 582 and 546; Solesmes, nos. 625 and 549).

The concern expressed in this maxim is easily linked to the Protestant error that wants only one Mediator and tolerates no secondary mediators.

– 9 –

When the faithful recite the divine office, they are performing a liturgical prayer.

Liturgical prayer, which is made in the name of the Church with the words and rites proposed by her, can only be made by priests or religious to whom it is incumbent. The prayer of the simple faithful is always a private prayer, whether its formula is liturgical or extra-liturgical.

Explanation

"The divine office is the prayer of the mystical Body of Christ addressed to God, in the name and for the benefit of all Christians, by priests and other ministers of the Church, as well as by religious, delegated by her for this purpose" (*Mediator Dei*, AAS 39, page 573; Solesmes, 601).

– 10 –

For their spiritual life and union with Jesus Christ, it is sufficient for the faithful to participate in liturgical acts by reciting the official texts.

The spiritual life of the faithful necessarily involves not only participation in Holy Mass and the sacraments, but also acts of private piety, without which salvation is impossible.

Explanation

The refuted proposition is condemned by *Mediator Dei* in these terms: "Some conclude from these [...] arguments that all Christian piety must be confined to the mystery of the Mystical Body of Christ, without any 'personal' or 'subjective' consideration; they therefore believe that other religious practices that are not strictly liturgical and performed outside of public worship should be neglected. [...] All will notice, however, that these conclusions about the two kinds of piety are completely fallacious, insidious, and harmful" (AAS 39, page 533).

Moreover, for priests themselves, who are capable of reciting proper liturgical prayers, the Code of Canon Law recommends fervent private piety (Can. 125, § 2).

– 11 –

It is retrograde moralism to forbid the faithful from attending balls, dance halls, and swimming pools. Nourished by liturgical piety, they can frequent these places without fear and practice the apostolate by infiltration, radiating Christ through their presence.

No spirituality immunizes man against the danger of proximate and voluntary occasions of sin, which must be avoided even at the cost of serious prejudice. Apostolate exercised with a proximate risk of losing oneself is reckless and cannot count on the blessings of the Lord.

Explanation

The erroneous proposition would be true if there existed a union (sacramental and vital) with God, obtained through the liturgy, that was not only superior to but unrelated to moral union with God; or, according to another hypothesis, if the life of grace were such that it dispensed human cooperation. But for those who profess authentic Catholic doctrine, neither of these assumptions can be accepted. Today, as always, the Holy See and moralists warn the faithful against entertainments that constitute proximate occasions of sin.

The refuted maxim recalls the quietism condemned by Innocent XI on August 28 and November 27, 1667. Among the condemned propositions is this one: "If, through one's own faults, one scandalizes others, it is not necessary to reflect on this as long as there is no intention to scandalize; and not being able to reflect on one's own faults is a grace from God"

(DS 2210). Thus, the refuted maxim presupposes automatic sanctification, without any contribution from the human will.

– 12 –

The state of marriage is placed above the state of perfect chastity because it is sanctified by a sacrament.

The degree of perfection of a state of life is measured by the degree of union with God, which is normally obtained through sanctifying grace and charity. That is why the most perfect state presupposes greater self-denial on the part of those who embrace it and must offer them greater means of sanctification. Thus, the state of perfection par excellence is the religious state, and the state of perfect chastity is higher than that of marriage.

Explanation

It cannot be said that every state that is constituted by a sacrament is, by that very fact, more perfect than another. Thus, although there is no special sacrament for the religious state, we know that Our Lord presented the practice of the evangelical counsels as the measure of perfection.

As for the superiority of virginity over marital continence, see chapter seven of the First Epistle to the Corinthians and, in St. Thomas' *Summa Theologica*, II-II, 152, a. 4, as well as II-II, q. 40, a. 2, ad 4. Moreover, virginity can be considered the fruit of the sacrament of the Eucharist, which makes it practicable for mortals.

The refuted maxim was censured several times by the Church. Thus: in the Syllabus of Pius IV, *the Nota bene* after proposition no. 74 (DN 2974) – in Pius XII's address to nuns in September 1952, where the Holy Father rebukes priests, lay people, preachers, orators, and writers who "no longer have a word of approval or praise for virginity consecrated to Christ; who, for years, despite the warnings of the Church and contrary to its thinking, have given marriage a preference in principle over virginity; who even go so far as to present it as the only means capable of ensuring the development and natural perfection of the human personality" (To the Superiors General of Women's Religious Orders and Congregations, Solesmes, *Les Instituts de vie parfaite*, 811). The same thoughts are found in the address of April 23, 1952, to a group of young girls, in which the pope repeats that the religious vocation will always remain a more perfect state than that of marriage.

It is not necessary to insist on the immense harm that these ideas cause in our diocese: the propaganda that Protestants spread against celibacy is one of the weapons with which heretics satisfy their hatred for everything that comes from the Church of God.

— 13 —

Since the parish is a community, the preservation of community life requires that all parishioners participate together in the same sacrifice, receive the graces of the same spiritual father, and unite their prayers in the same temple. The fact that the faithful attend other parishes or non-parish churches breaks the unity of community life.
The parish is the cell of the diocese, and therefore it is necessary that all parishioners maintain lively contact with their parish priest and place themselves under his guidance. But such contact and guidance are entirely compatible with the faithful receiving the sacraments and attending Holy Mass in other churches. Therefore, these practices should not be prohibited or discouraged.

Explanation

If by community life we mean the communion of the faithful in the same supernatural mysteries, this communion loses none of its intensity when parishioners participate in these mysteries in different churches. If by community life we mean a certain natural familiarity that leads to virtue, such familiarity is also possible for the faithful in a church other than their parish church. For a person, attending the church of a religious convent, for example, while maintaining ties with the edifying faithful of his parish or other parishes, can only be beneficial, and the spiritual advantages he receives from this necessarily have a beneficial influence on his own parish.

The action of religious and rectors of non-parish churches will be very effective in ensuring a correct understanding of this question, if they instruct the faithful on their duties towards their parish and their parish priest, and if they are always eager to help parish priests in everything related to parish life.

Since, in general, a Jansenist influence can be perceived in all these errors, we should recall here that it was the intrigues of the Jansenists that brought this "parochial spirit" into vogue, a spirit that reigned in Paris in the 17th century and prepared parish priests to take the constitutional oath at the time of the French Revolution. It was the same spirit that, in Pistoia, dictated restrictive rules on the activities of religious, which Pope Pius VI fortunately condemned.

However, parishioners who are completely ignorant of their parish priest would be blameworthy. For the latter must be kept informed of the fulfillment of the religious duties of all his parishioners. This is clear from the Code of Canon Law, which, in canon 859, advises the faithful to celebrate Easter in their own parish and asks them, if they do not do so, to inform their parish priest.

The refuted maxim would be best reconciled with an "ontological" conception of the parish community, according to which, through participation in liturgical functions, parishioners would be absorbed into a single essential whole of a higher order: the mystical and communal Christ. The "ontological" parish community would continue even in the temporal realm, making the parish a whole in which families and properties would merge completely or almost completely, in a quasi-biological communion of all kinds of goods. Even in the temporal order, individual personalities would thus merge into a single collective personality.

But if we understand community not as an ontological reality, but as a moral reality, albeit supernaturalized by grace, the erroneous maxim becomes unfounded.

II — On the Structure of the Church

— 14 —

Within the diocese, the only authentic interpreter of the acts of the Holy See is the diocesan bishop. Thus, the faithful and the ordinary priest can never deviate from his interpretation.

The interpretation of pontifical acts belongs solely to the Holy See. No other interpretation, however respectable and learned it may be, can be imposed as official and unique.

Explanation

See *Directive* No. 8, which reads as follows:[16]

On the ecclesiastical magisterium, teach that since the papal magisterium is infallible and that of each bishop is official but fallible, it is in the nature of human frailty that one bishop or another may fall into error. History records such occurrences. They produce, as one might expect, the most dangerous consequences. Nevertheless, it is necessary to teach the faithful how they should act in such circumstances. In such painful cases, the first duty of the faithful is to maintain all due respect for the sacred person of the pastor given to them by Providence and to faithfully carry out his orders in everything that does not hinder the direct and higher fidelity they owe to the Vicar of Christ.

---

16 These are the Directives of Bishop de Castro-Mayer to his clergy, published on the same day and appended to the Catechism of Truths. See at the end.

— 15 —

The union of the faithful with the Pope is realized in the person of the bishop. Those who follow the opinions of their ordinary completely can be certain that they are in absolute conformity with the mind of the Holy See.

The bishop has the ordinary magisterium, so that the faithful must receive his teaching as the faithful expression of the mind of the Church. However, by a disposition of Jesus Christ, the official magisterium of the bishop is not infallible when exercised in isolation. Consequently, the faithful cannot bring the same degree of submission to the bishop's magisterium as to that of the pope, although they must, in a just measure, respect and obey both.

Explanation

Guideline No. 7:

Never miss an opportunity to teach true devotion to the Holy Father, the Pope, and, to a lesser degree, to the diocesan bishop.

On this point, it is necessary to avoid a certain tendency which, with the laudable aim of strengthening the bonds of charity between the sheep and the local pastor, presents the bishop in such a light as to confer on him a kind of infallibility, almost making him equal to the Holy Father, who, according to this conception, would be merely a censor of the bishops. Therefore, teach the correct doctrine concerning the relationship between the pope and the bishops.

Our Lord Jesus Christ instituted in the Church a single hierarchy of government, consisting of two degrees that are in harmony: the pope and, subordinate to him, the bishops (CIC, can. 108, § 3).[17] The unity of this hierarchy is an indispensable concept for the faithful to know how to position themselves in relation to it. By seeing it as a single whole, with the Supreme

17 "by reason of jurisdiction, [the sacred hierarchy consists of] the supreme pontificate and the subordinate Episcopate."

Pontiff at its summit, the source of all jurisdiction in the Church, and by considering the bishops and the Pope in the same perspective, the faithful will show them all the respect, veneration, and love they owe them.

In this vein, it should be remembered that fullness of power belongs to the Roman Pontiff, who has direct and immediate jurisdiction over the bishops and all the faithful. The jurisdiction of the bishops, successors of the apostles, is exercised in harmony with and under the authority of the pontifical jurisdiction.

Such is the natural framework of the Church. To seek to instill a devotion to the pope that is entirely different from and even opposed to devotion to the bishop, and vice versa, to seek to instill a devotion to the bishop that is different from and even opposed to devotion to the pope, would be to implicitly deny the harmonious unity of the hierarchy. Let us love the pope and the bishop with extreme charity and devotion, each according to his rank and in proportion to the powers conferred on them by Our Lord Jesus Christ.

The faithful most devoted to his bishop — and every Catholic must be so — will have no fear of showing great respect for the supreme authority of the Roman Pontiff, in all the extent conferred on him by the divine founder of the Church.

− 16 −

By joining Catholic Action organizations, the faithful receive a share in the apostolic mandate and hierarchical functions, which enables them to carry out a specifically priestly apostolate.

The Church is, by divine institution, an unequal society in which there is a distinction between those who teach and those who are taught: the hierarchy and the subjects. The members of Catholic Action organizations belong entirely to the category of subjects, that is, to the taught Church. They therefore have no share in the teaching function or hierarchical power. Their actions are specifically the same as those of any other faithful.

Explanation

The mandate conferred by Our Lord Jesus Christ on the apostles and their successors concerns everything related to the salvation of souls. Members of the various degrees of the hierarchy participate—in the true and proper sense of the term—in this mandate, which implies the power to govern, teach, and sanctify.

The laity cannot, as such, receive any part of hierarchical power. Certainly, they participate in the work of the hierarchy and collaborate with it. But it is obvious that they do not participate in its powers. Even when a father teaches catechism to his children or when a commissioned catechist provides religious instruction, one cannot speak, either properly or in any sense whatsoever, of participation in the teaching power of the Church. The father and the catechist are collaborators with the hierarchy, but they do not cease to belong entirely to the Taught Church.

All the documents of the Holy See on Catholic Action consider the question in this way, as is natural, since it is the only one that is appropriate to the divine institution of the Church.

This is what Pius XI said in his address to Catholic journalists on July 26, 1929: "... Catholic journalists are numerous spokesmen for the Church, its hierarchy, and its teaching; consequently, they are the most distinguished and devoted spokesmen for everything that the Holy Mother Church says and does. In fulfilling this function, the Catholic press does not belong to the Teaching Church; it continues to be part of the Taught Church; and yet, everywhere, it is nonetheless the messenger of the discipline of the Teaching Church, of that Church charged with teaching the nations of the world."

This is an observation whose importance cannot be overemphasized. While, on the one hand, pontifical documents point out and condemn various errors that have arisen in connection with Catholic Action, on the other hand, they express the greatest desire to preserve and expand this association. There is no contradiction between these two attitudes. If the Holy See corrects dangerous deviations relating to Catholic Action, it is precisely because it desires that it develop in rectitude and effectiveness. It is in this position of balance that those who devote themselves to this field must also maintain themselves.

— 17 —

Catholic Action and the diocesan clergy are organizations instituted by the Church and, as such, exercise an official apostolate; religious congregations and other associations are particular institutions approved by the Church, which exercise an unofficial apostolate.

In the Church, the priestly state is distinguished from the lay state as being specifically superior to it. For its part, the religious state is itself superior to the secular state. Thus, the priestly apostolate has preeminence over all others, and the apostolate of religious has preeminence over that of the laity.

Explanation

The refuted sentence gives the apostolate of the laity in Catholic Action an official status and the apostolate of religious a merely unofficial and therefore inferior status, which is contrary to the order of values.

— 18 —

Since it gives participation in the hierarchical apostolate, membership in Catholic Action confers on the faithful a grace of state which, by that very fact, makes their apostolate more effective than that exercised by members of other associations.

Participation in the hierarchical apostolate, by which Pope Pius XI defined Catholic Action, does not imply, for the laity, a special status in the Church, distinct from that of other faithful who are not enrolled in the main associations of Catholic Action. This is why membership in Catholic Action does not confer on a person any grace specifically different from that received by lay people who are members of other apostolic associations.

Explanation

The refuted statement presupposes an intermediate status between the teaching Church and the taught Church. This would justify a specific grace of status, more effective in itself than that of ordinary members of the taught Church.

— 19 —

The main Catholic Action organizations are approved and encouraged by the Holy See. Other associations (Apostleship of Prayer, Children of Mary, Marian congregations, etc.) are merely tolerated. In the spirit of the Holy See, they should gradually disappear.

> Marian congregations and other associations which, like them, have an apostolic form and purpose, belong by right to Catholic Action. Other associations are providential auxiliaries of Catholic Action and should therefore be encouraged because of the great services they are called to render to the Church.

Explanation

In the apostolic constitution *Bis saeculari die* of September 27, 1948, on Marian congregations (AAS, vol. 40, page 393 ff.), Pope Pius XII taught emphatically and very solemnly that Catholic Action cannot be organized in the standardized and totalitarian manner of modern states.[18]

That is why he places Marian congregations and other associations that pursue an apostolic goal, although diverse in spirit, constitution, and activity, on the same level as the main organizations of Catholic Action. And, for the same reason, the pontiff is pleased to note the great abundance of religious associations other than Catholic Action.

---

18 The Holy See has declared many times: "Catholic Action [...] does not claim to achieve its goal by any particular means or method" (Pius XI, Letter *Quæ nobis* to Cardinal Bertram, Nov. 13, 1928, AAS 20, 1928, p. 386), to the point of suppressing or absorbing other active Catholic associations; rather, it will consider its role to be "to unite them, to find amicable arrangements, to make the progress of one benefit the others, in perfect harmony, in union and charity" (Pius XI, *Address to Catholic Action in France*, May 20, 1931). Indeed, as we recently recommended in explicit terms, [...] "we must avoid the error of some who want to reduce everything that is undertaken for the good of souls to a single formula" (Pius XII, *Radio message to the International Congress of Marian Congregations in Barcelona*, December 7, 1947, AAS 39, 1947, p. 364); for, it must be said, "this way of acting is completely at odds with the spirit of the Church" (Pius XI, *Address to Italian Catholic Action*, June 28, 1930). [...] Congregations must be placed on the same level as other associations pursuing an apostolic goal." (*Pontifical Documents of His Holiness Pius XII*, 1948, Paris-Louvain, Labergerie-Warny, pp. 336-351.)

— 20 —

The legal nature of Catholic Action is such that the ceremony for the admission of its members can only be presided over by the bishop or one of his delegates.

Catholic Action being an organization that falls entirely under the authority of the Church, its members must normally be received by the vicar or by the priest who directs the group.

Explanation

The refuted statement would be true if Catholic Action constituted an intermediate degree between the Teaching Church and the Taught Church.

— 21 —

The legal nature of Catholic Action is such that the ecclesiastical assistant exercises no authority over it, except in a negative sense, since he can veto the deliberations of the leadership when they contain anything contrary to faith or morals. All authority belongs to the laity, who regard the priest as a mere director of conscience.

Catholic Action, belonging to the Taught Church, is entirely subject to the authority of the bishop, whose official representative is the ecclesiastical assistant; the latter's authority is exercised not only to prohibit anything contrary to faith and morals, but also to govern all social activity. In Catholic Action, as in other associations, the ecclesiastical assistant will exercise his functions with charity, giving lay people the consideration they deserve and taking into account their valuable experience.

Explanation

If the priest had only a simple power of veto over Catholic Action, it would practically escape the bishop's authority. On the other hand, the rejected proposal would only be justified if Catholic Action were something specifically superior to the Taught Church, in a situation parallel to that of ordinary priests.

— 22 —

The apostolate in the community (universities, neighborhoods, etc.) is specific to Catholic Action. Since the priest does not belong to these communities, he is unable to direct the specific apostolate of Catholic Action.

Apostolate in the community is an obligation for all the faithful. To lead the apostolate of the faithful, Jesus Christ instituted the sacred hierarchy. By virtue of their position, through special studies, and by rising above the particularities of each milieu in order to have an overview of them, the members of the hierarchy have all the resources necessary to carry out their mission. The prudent priest will know how to use, in his leadership role, the valuable contribution of the experience that lay people have in their respective milieus.

Explanation

The function of government is necessarily at a general and higher level. United with the ecclesiastical leadership, lay people can provide it with the assistance of "experts" because they are familiar with all the particularities of the respective environments in which they live. As devoted, disinterested, and valuable advisors, but only advisors, they must be ready to follow obediently the orders of the priest and the direction he gives to the activities of the group.

The priest's inability to know the environments in which the lay apostolate is exercised was explicitly denied by the Holy Father in his closing address at the first World Congress of the Lay Apostolate (AAS, vol. 43, pages 789-790) on October 14, 1951, when he said: "The call for the cooperation of the laity is not due to the failure or shortcoming of the clergy in their present task. " And, in a positive way: "The priest has as good eyes as the lay person to discern the signs of the times, and his ear is no less sensitive to the auscultation of the human heart." To leave no doubt, the Pope gave the reason for this collaboration with the laity: "The laity are called to the apostolate as collaborators with the priest [...] because of the shortage of clergy, who are too few in number."[19]

The apostolate of the laity in their milieu cannot be the exclusive privilege of Catholic Action, for it is the duty of every faithful to be an apostle in the milieu in which he lives. In twenty centuries of existence, the sacred hierarchy has been able to competently direct this apostolate. It is not clear how Catholic Action could bring about innovation on this particular point.

In other words, it is important not to view this question from a purely natural perspective. The Supreme Pontiff has previously stated that the apostolate of Catholic Action is of an instructional nature, that the laity must be subordinate to the authority of the priest, the normal representative of the bishop. The instrumentality of the laity in the apostolate must always be understood, of course, in a sense that is appropriate to human persons and not to inanimate beings. The Holy Father has said that "ecclesiastical superiors use him [the lay person] in the same way that the Creator and Lord uses rational creatures, as instruments, as secondary causes, 'with great favour' (Wisdom 12:18)."[20] Such is the plan of Providence, which dispenses its grace only to what is done according to the divine constitution of the Church.

---

19 *Pontifical Documents of His Holiness Pius XII*, 1951, Paris, Labergerie, p. 427.
20 Pius XII, *Address to participants in the First Congress of the Lay Apostolate*, October 14, 1951, ibid., p. 426

— 23 —

In Catholic Action, interior formation is provided by the apostolate itself, which dispenses with other means traditionally employed.

The apostolate of Catholic Action presupposes the careful use of all the traditional means of interior formation as a condition for the perseverance and sanctification of its members and the fruitfulness of their activities.

Explanation

The refuted statement seems to stem from the idea that Catholic Action is something entirely new in the Church, creating its own system of spirituality. Priests themselves are not exempt from using traditional means of spiritual formation. It is difficult to understand how members of Catholic Action could do without them, unless one assumes that Catholic Action has a spirituality that is opposed to that which the Church has always taught.

— 24 —

In recruiting activists and leaders for Catholic Action, it is necessary, with a view to the apostolate of conquest, to favor natural aptitudes and technical training rather than grace and supernatural formation.

By a mysterious design of Providence, natural qualities and divine grace contribute to the apostolate. Since divine grace is the indispensable and preponderant element, in choosing apostles, one must first take into account their spiritual formation.

Explanation

This refuted proposition also stems from the idea that Catholic Action constitutes something entirely new within the Church, and this is not in keeping with its true traditions.

— 25 —

The best method of formation consists of "study circles" in which truth arises spontaneously from conversation among the participants, without the need for a superior teacher to lecture them on the subject.

The normal method of teaching, especially when it comes to revealed truths, is that of the "magisterium:" a more knowledgeable and authorized person lectures on the subject to others who listen.

Explanation

Study circles, in the form envisaged by the refuted proposal, were condemned by St. Pius X in his Letter on the *Sillon*.[21] Indeed, this form is revolutionary in inspiration and tends to suppress the authority of the teacher.

— 26 —

The apostolate of conquest (attracting unbelievers and those who habitually live in a state of sin) is the apostolate par excellence. The apostolate of preserving and encouraging the good is secondary.

---

21 "Study circles are true intellectual cooperatives, where everyone is both teacher and student. [...] Even the priest, when he enters, lowers the eminent dignity of his priesthood and, in the strangest reversal of roles, becomes a student, placing himself on the same level as his young friends and becoming nothing more than a comrade " (Letter "*Notre Charge Apostolique*" from our Holy Father Pope Pius X to the French episcopate on "*Le Sillon*," *Acts of His Holiness Pius X*, Paris, *Éditions de la Documentation catholique*, vol. V, p. 133).

> Our greatest obligations of charity are towards those who live most united to God. Therefore, our zeal must be directed first and foremost towards preserving the good. Furthermore, the formation of fervent lay people is an indispensable condition for a true apostolate of conquest, which we must all encourage.

Explanation

Both apostolates are essential: preserving and perfecting the good, and converting sinners. Moreover, it is a mistake to dissociate the apostolate of preserving and encouraging the good from the apostolate of winning souls. The former is the condition for the latter. The divine Master prepared for the conversion of the world by forming a handful of fervent apostles. In other words, it is impossible to win over the masses without first forming an elite.

− 27 −

> In the current circumstances, where the apostolate is a necessity, it would be better that purely contemplative religious families cease to exist, or see a significant reduction in their membership; indeed, by devoting themselves exclusively to penance and prayer, these people render themselves useless for the active external apostolate.

> By divine providence, the conquest of souls is achieved by two means: on the one hand, by the external and visible activity of the hierarchy and the faithful, and on the other hand, by the internal and invisible action of grace, based largely on the prayer and reparative penance of contemplatives.

Explanation

Pope Pius XII, in view of the current situation in the world, has granted facilities to contemplatives to enable them to exercise an active apostolate as well. However, this does not mean the suppression of contemplative religious families, nor a reduction that would amount to something similar. Moreover, in the same document, the Holy Father emphasizes that this apostolate must in no way dispense with the contemplative life or diminish its intensity. Here are his words:

"Et in primis, quoad vitam monialium contemplativam, hoc, quod juxta mentem Ecclesiæ semper viguit, firmum ac inviolatum servari debet: Monasteria omnia monialium vitam contemplativam, ut primum atque præcipuum suum finem, canonice semper et ubique profiteri debere. Quam ob rem, labores et ministeria, quibus moniales vacare possunt ac debent, talia esse oportet atque ita quoad locum, tempus, modum rationemque ordinanda ac disponenda sunt ut vita vere et solide contemplativa, sive totius communitatis, sive singularum monialium, salva non tantum sit, sed jugiter alatur ac roboretur" (Apostolic Constitution *Sponsa Christi*, November 21, 1950, concerning the status of nuns, AAS 43, page 11).

"First of all, with regard to the contemplative life of nuns, this, which has always been in force, according to the spirit of the Church, must be maintained firmly and intact: all monasteries of nuns must always and everywhere regularly profess the contemplative life as their first and principal end. Therefore, the works and ministries to which nuns can and must devote themselves must be of such a nature and arranged in such a way in terms of place, time, measure, and manner that the truly and sincerely contemplative life of the whole community, as well as of each individual nun, is not only safeguarded but also constantly nourished and strengthened."[22]

---

22 *Pontifical Documents of His Holiness Pius XII*, 1950, Paris, Labergerie, p. 549.

— 28 —

> The clergyman's suit is more appropriate for our times. It makes the apostolate easier than the cassock reaching down to the heels, which is required by canon law.

Since the priest, through the sacrament of Holy Orders, is a consecrated person and occupies a specifically distinct position in the Church, placed above the common faithful, it is highly appropriate and in keeping with his position that he should have an outfit completely different from that which the simple faithful are accustomed to wearing.

Explanation

The Church has always preferred the use of the cassock. The clergyman's attire, on the other hand, comes from countries where the situation created by heresy and persecution has made it difficult for priests to lead the normal life they lead in Catholic countries. It is therefore in keeping with the spirit of the Church to praise and preserve the cassock. It is on the basis of this preference for the cassock that the collective pastoral letter of the Brazilian episcopate, reissued with a new approval by all the bishops in 1950,[23] imposes its use under severe penalties (no. 1262)[24] and tolerates other clothing only

---

23 See additional note after the end of the article.

24 "Clerics who do not wear long garments or the clerical tonsure will be *severely admonished*. One month after the admonition, if it has had no effect, clerics in minor orders who have acted in this way without legitimate cause shall *ipso facto* lose all rights to clerical orders; those in holy orders shall be suspended from the orders received and shall *ipso facto*, without any declaration, lose all ecclesiastical offices they held; and if they notoriously pass to another state of life, foreign to the clerical state, and, after being admonished again, do not repent, they shall be deposed three months after the last admonition" (CIC 136, § 3; 188, n. 7; 2379). (The italics are those of the official text.)

in special circumstances (No. 1260[25] and 1261).[26] Canon 136 of the Code requires priests to have special clothing, but it shows a preference for the cassock when it orders them to wear it to celebrate Holy Mass (canon 811).[27] This preference for the cassock is explained: The cassock, which is quite different from ordinary civilian clothing, better marks the separation between the priest and secular life than the clergyman's attire. The abolition of the cassock has a very strong impact on the secularization of the clergy.

— 29 —

It is more in keeping with the current needs of the Holy Church that priests, in their social life, allow themselves all the entertainment that is permitted to lay Catholics, as well as ways of life that are not forbidden to the latter.

Each state of life has not only its duties, but also its appropriate ways of being and behaving. Therefore, a good priest will refrain not only from what morality expressly condemns, but also from anything that, according to the established expression, *non clericat* [is not fitting to clerics].

Explanation

The essential rules of morality cannot be reduced to what a man may or may not do. Thus, the behavior, leisure activities, and ways of being permitted to a manual laborer are not appropriate for a magistrate; a head of a family does not allow

---

25 "When traveling on horseback, although the cassock is always preferable, we tolerate the short cassock, called a "levite," that is, a kind of black or other colored frock coat, closed to the collar and reaching to the knees, with a collar and soft felt hat. It is understood, however, that the 'levite' is tolerated only during the journey itself and is not permitted in any other circumstances."

26 "When traveling abroad, we allow secular clothing, but only in regions where the use of long garments is prohibited, and even then, with due precautions."

27 The celebrant must wear suitable clothing reaching down to the heels.

himself the conduct and ways of a young bachelor, even if the latter fully respects the prescriptions of morality. To abolish the manners, behaviors, and lifestyle proper to the priesthood and to encourage priests to lead an honest life, but one similar to that of the laity, is to work toward the secularization of society and, worse still, the secularization of the Church. On this subject, see canon 138[28] of the Code of Canon Law.

— 30 —

The atmosphere of majesty and aristocratic distinction that surrounds the hierarchy is an imitation of temporal princes. However, the bishop is a pastor, not a prince. Therefore, what befits him is not the appearance of a prince, but the simplicity and poverty of a pastor.

Because man has a sensitive nature, it is necessary that external appearances reveal the intimate nature of institutions. That is why the higher the office, the more solemn the atmosphere surrounding it must be. The bishop has the dignity of a prince in the Church of God. And ecclesiastical principality is a more eminent dignity than civil principality. Therefore, he has an obligation to surround himself with the splendor befitting his office. But in his private life, he must excel in practicing detachment from all earthly things.

Explanation

The refuted sentence is impressive for its play on words. It makes the bishop a pastor, but it insinuates an identity between two conditions, when there is only an analogy between them. The pastoral ministry of men has a dignity

28 "Clerics shall entirely abstain from all those things that are indecent to their state; they shall not engage in indecorous arts; they shall abstain from gambling games with risks of money; they shall not carry arms, except when there is just cause for fearing; hunting should not be indulged, and [then] never with clamor; taverns and similar places should not be entered without necessity or another just cause approved by the local Ordinary."

that is obviously superior to the government of sheep. It would therefore be contrary to the order of things for a prince or a bishop to present himself, in all respects, as a shepherd of sheep. Indirectly, this would reduce men to the rank of animals. It is quite obvious that episcopal splendor is in no way incompatible with the gentleness, humility, detachment, and paternal affability that should distinguish the bishop. Thus, the true bishop, while preserving the dignity of his office, will be the father of all and each of his diocesans.

— 31 —

The only way to understand and support the working class is for the priest to go out to the masses, mingle with them, adopt their ways, their manner of being and living, etc., in order to be able to exert an influence on this milieu.

Knowledge of the working class and the moral and religious problems that concern them requires a certain amount of living in common with them, and the exercise of parish ministry in the parish normally provides priests with excellent opportunities for this. In the presbytery or outside , the priest must be entirely and exclusively a priest, and refrain from all associations and behaviors that "*non clericant*."[29] For the rest, he will act through lay people affiliated with various Catholic Action groups, Marian congregations, etc., and through specialized associations such as workers' circles.

Explanation

The refuted sentence, with rare exceptions, reverses the roles: the priest leaves the presbytery and takes on the normal tasks of the laity. It is, moreover, a manifestation of the tendency toward the secularization of the clergy.

To understand what is one-sided about this proposal, it should be noted that it considers only the conversion of the

---

29 That is to say "unclerical" or not suitable for a priest.

working class, as if Paganism had not also wreaked terrible havoc in other social classes. Now, if we accept the principle that each class can only be approached by priests who belong to it, we should logically have farmer priests, industrial priests, military priests, diplomat priests, etc., and the only thing missing would be priest priests. The saints have always feared this kind of secularized life for themselves and for the clergy. And the Church has always recommended that priests guard against it with great care.

III- On Methods Of Apostolate
Irenicism — Interconfessionalism — Common ground — Polemics, etc.

— 32 —

It is more important to keep souls united in charity than united in truth.

Union in charity is the natural fruit of union in truth. Therefore, it is important above all to maintain the integrity of the faith, without which no one can please God (St. Paul to the Hebrews, 11:6).

Explanation

If we accept something more fundamental than faith, we necessarily fall into the conclusion that the difference between religions is secondary and, as a result, a whole interconfessional practice is justified. In reality, unity in faith is so crucial that we must give it an essential and dominant place in our relationships, not only with people outside the Church, but also with the Church's own children. We owe them a special charity. But if they use their status as Catholics to spread error within the Church, they must be the object of our lively and special opposition. It goes without saying that even in the heat of battle, charity must be preserved.

Moreover, if the objection were accepted, all the struggles, sometimes centuries-long, that the Church has waged to preserve the integrity of the faith within her would be inexplicable. When we consider that these struggles have led to persecutions, martyrdoms, and breaks within the mystical Body of Christ, we understand the paramount importance that Our Lord Jesus Christ attached to the integrity of the sacred deposit he entrusted to his Church.

— 33 —

Heretics and sinners—who are often well-intentioned people, but who are mistaken in their assessment of truth and goodness—must never be fought or attacked, at least not directly, in their ideas and morals. Such an approach would necessarily alienate and revolt them. On the contrary, whenever they are gently enlightened, they renounce their error and convert.

God has given everyone the grace to recognize truth and goodness, so that errors committed in good faith on this point are accidental and abnormal. In relations with heretics and sinners, true Christian leniency, which does not imply any condescension in matters of faith and morals, is certainly the most effective and, in itself, preferable. But when obstinacy resists the gentle and persuasive action of charity, when insolence causes scandal among the faithful, the use of energetic and combative methods is necessary.

Explanation

The refuted proposition is flawed by its oversimplification and lack of nuance. It is certain that there are heretics, infidels, and sinners who may be attracted by Christian gentleness. It would be a manifest error to act with unnecessary harshness in dealing with them. However, there are also heretics and sinners (and in certain periods, they were unfortunately very numerous) who are only moved by the energetic condemnation of their error and under the influence of a salutary fear, as they become aware of their condition. This was the case with David when he was rebuked by the prophet Nathan.

In this matter, we must also take into account the diversity of temperaments. To convert the Apostle of the Gentiles [St. Paul], Providence, always full of love, deemed it necessary to throw him to the ground.

Ultimately, the choice of methods of apostolate must not be inspired solely by the convenience of the heretic or sinner, but must consider above all the salvation and edification of those who live in the grace of God. When a heretic or sinner, instead of humbly keeping in the shadows, flaunts his error or even spreads it by word and example, it is often necessary to compel him by force. The Holy Scriptures are full of examples that support this doctrine. This is how Jesus Christ acted with the scribes and Pharisees, St. Peter with Ananias and Sapphira, St. Paul with the incestuous in Corinth, etc.

— 34 —

Hate the error, love those who err, says St. Augustine. Therefore, we must attack only errors and sins, never those who err or those who sin.
Hate error, love those who err, says St. Augustine. We must therefore attack error or sin: by expounding Catholic doctrine, by combating false doctrines, and by warning the faithful against those who err or sin. There is no lack of charity in this, for it is an act of mercy to correct those who err and to prevent the spread of error.

Explanation

The refuted maxim seems to assume that any punishment of those who err is an act of hostility toward them. The Church teaches, on the contrary, that punishing the guilty is, in itself, an act of mercy. This would not be the case if this course of action were dictated by hatred, envy, or a spirit of defamation, or if it were excessive or inappropriate.

Moreover, the entire history of the Church, even before its foundation, from its origins to the time of its last doctors — St. Francis de Sales, for example — is filled with vehement condemnations of sinners and heretics. Let us recall St. John the Baptist's *"genimina viperarum* [generation of vipers]" directed at the Pharisees (Lk 3:7), the "whited sepulchres" and other "hypocrites" (Mt 23:27) that Jesus Christ hurled at this same category of people, etc.

— 35 —

In relations with infidels and sinners, it is preferable to remain silent about the truths of Catholic doctrine to which they are opposed and about the austerity of the moral precepts they transgress, and to emphasize mainly the truths they profess and the sweetness of the Gospel precepts. It is by remaining on common ground with both groups that Catholics are able to attract the sympathy of infidels and sinners and convert them.

The doctrine and morals of the Church are perfect and capable of arousing the admiration of men, both in their demanding requirements and in their consoling principles. Moreover, no man lacks the inner help of grace. Certainly, when dealing with stubborn minds, it is more appropriate to emphasize the truths and precepts that are most easily acceptable, but these are exceptional situations. Normally, it is necessary to insist on all points of Catholic doctrine.

Explanation

The objection is flawed by Naturalism, because it ignores the divine grace that makes the cross of Jesus Christ lovable. It was by preaching Jesus Christ crucified that the apostles conquered the world, not by using the tactic of "common ground" [seeking what unites us and remaining silent about what separates us]. This is the doctrine of St. Pius X, as can be verified in the encyclical *Jucunda sane* published on the occasion of the thirteenth centenary of the death of St. Gregory the Great. In it, the pope praises this saint, especially because he disregarded the advice dictated by carnal prudence, presenting himself with the austerity of a preacher of Christ crucified, as the apostles had already done, in the midst of a cultured, civilized, and brilliant Rome: preaching to such an audience in the name of a man condemned to death on a cross seemed totally doomed to failure.

We can also read propositions 93 and 94 (DS2493 and 2494) of Quesnel, condemned by Clement XI. They praise gentleness and charity in defiance of firmness in the faith.[30]

— 36 —

Controversy between Catholics, or between Catholics and non-Catholics, necessarily sacrifices charity and is always wrong. Those who engage in controversy, if they are not heretics in the order of truth, are heretics in the order of charity.

Just and timely controversy is one of the means of promoting charity, contributing to the unity of minds in truth. Refusing to engage in controversy may, in certain cases, constitute what is rightly called a "heresy" against charity.

Explanation

The objection assumes that dogmatic differences are to be disregarded, since it is differences of this kind that give rise to polemics. This mental attitude, which characterizes the "Irenicist," can lead to a theoretical inter-confessionalism with disastrous repercussions in the practical order, for it naturally leads to religious indifferentism. This error is implicitly condemned by the censure of Quesnel's proposition 94, as we have seen above, because this proposition criticizes the Holy Church for its firmness, whereas, as the history of its firmness in the faith shows, the Jansenists reproached the Holy See for being excessive in its practical demands.

---

30 Proposition 93 (condemned): "Jesus sometimes heals the wounds inflicted by the hastiness of the first pastors without his command; Jesus restores what they cut away through ill-considered zeal." Proposition 94 (condemned): "Nothing gives a worse opinion of the Church to its enemies than to see it exercising dominion over the faith of the faithful and maintaining divisions over matters that do not harm either faith or morals."

If the refuted proposition were true, the struggle against the Church's external adversaries and especially against its internal enemies, who, disguised as sheep, seek to decimate the flock, would prove impossible. Saint Pius X, in a letter to His Eminence Cardinal Ferrari, Archbishop of Milan, shows how harmful such a course of action can be to the Church: he denounces "... those who repeat in their writings all the errors of Modernism, who feign outward submission in order to remain in the fold and more surely propagate their errors, who continue their harmful work through secret readings and congresses, and who, in a word, betray the Church by pretending to be her friends. [...] Who cannot see the sad impression and scandal caused to souls by considering as Catholics these wretched people whom, by order of the Apostle St. John, we should refuse to greet?"[31]

— 37 —

Every effort must be made to silence those who show intransigence in defending Catholic doctrine. There is no error more pernicious than that of intransigence in the truth.

Intransigence is to virtue what the instinct for self-preservation is to life. A faith without intransigence, or who hates intransigence, does not exist or retains only the appearance of existence. A faith without intransigence is either already dead or lives only outwardly, for it has lost the spirit [of faith]. Faith being the foundation of supernatural life, tolerance in matters of faith is the starting point of all evils, especially heresies.

Explanation

St. Pius X pointed out that one of the characteristics of Modernists is extreme tolerance towards the enemies of the Church and bitter intolerance towards those who vigorously

31 *Disquisitio or: investigation of the beatification and canonization processes of St. Pius X;* in: *Conduct of St. Pius X in the fight against modernism,* Versailles, publications of the *Courrier de Rome,* 1996, pp. 171-172.

defend orthodoxy. In reality, there is a flagrant inconsistency in this attitude, for those who claim to tolerate all opinions should tolerate those who uphold the rights of intransigence. This contradiction is common to all heresiarchs. The various sects unite with great cordiality and turn a blind eye to their points of divergence whenever it comes to combating the Church's intransigence in matters of faith. This attitude provides us with a criterion for judging the singular importance of intolerance in doctrinal matters in the life of the Church.[32]

It is obvious that excesses of intransigence, precisely because they are excesses, must be repressed, for all excess is evil. Nevertheless, it is important not to forget the wise norms dictated by the Holy See, under the pontificate of St. Pius X, on how to correct this or that excess committed by courageous Catholic polemicists engaged in the fight against error. Writing to Cardinal Ferrari, Archbishop of Milan, about the newspaper *La Riscossa*, which was alarmed by the modernist infiltration within that archdiocese, His Eminence Cardinal De Lai, secretary of the Sacred Consistorial Congregation, said:

"All these facts taken together explain why there are good people who fear for their beloved diocese and raise their voices in alarm. Perhaps they exaggerate in their manner. But in battle, who can seriously accuse the defenders if they do not calculate their blows accurately and perhaps exceed the limits of *inculpatæ tutelæ* [irreproachable defense]? This was how St. Jerome responded to those who reproached him for his zeal against the heretics and unbelievers of his time.

"This is also what I will say to Your Eminence regarding the attack on *La Riscossa*. After the cases cited above [Modernism in Milan], one cannot deny that evil exists. Therefore, it is not surprising, and one cannot say that it is totally unjust, that some have raised their voices. Have they exaggerated in their methods? But it is excusable, and it is not entirely wrong, if, in

---

32 On this question, see Cardinal Pie's text: "*Doctrinal Intolerance.*"

sounding the alarm, the danger was exaggerated. It is always better to exaggerate in warning of evil than to remain silent and let it grow."[33]

A little further on, the same letter continued:

"Finally, in the face of such license on the part of the bad press, and in view of the real dangers surrounding the Church on all sides, it does not seem right to tie the hands of its defenders, nor to strike them down and disavow them at every little mistake."[34]

And the holy pope himself, writing on August 12, 1909, to Archbishop Mistrangelo of Florence, regarding a change that had been ordered in the editorial policy of the Catholic newspaper *L'Unità Cattolica*, declared:

"It seems to me, based on this long conversation, that I see in him [lawyer Calligari, director of *L'Unità Cattolica*] a man of peace [...] who agrees wholeheartedly when it comes to respecting people. But I would not want, for the sake of peace, to see compromises being made and, in order to avoid trouble, the true mission of *L'Unità Cattolica* being diminished, which is to uphold principles, to be an advanced sentinel capable of sounding the alarm (just like the Capitoline goose) and to wake up those who are asleep. In that case, *L'Unità* would no longer have a reason to exist."[35]

— 38 —

We should praise Catholics who join with people of other religions, even Protestants, schismatics, etc., to defend values common to all Christian denominations.

---

33 *Disquisitio, Conduct of Saint Pius X in the Fight Against Modernism,* Versailles, publications of *Courrier de Rome*, 1996, p. 182
34 *Ibid.*
35 *Ibid.*, p. 137.

> The collaboration of the faithful with non-Catholics to achieve common goals is permitted by the Church only on an occasional basis. Much more dangerous would be for Catholics to associate with people of other religions on a permanent basis within the same organization. The Church views such associations with apprehension and forbids them. When, in exceptional circumstances, in order to avoid greater evils, she feels obliged to tolerate collaborations of this nature, she does so with fear and regret.

Explanation

The danger of such collaborations can be aggravated by the specific purpose they serve: thus, a collaboration of an exclusively technical-professional nature is less serious than a collaboration that pursues a cultural goal. The "Christian Youth Association," for example, was banned by the Church because, bringing together Christians of various sects, it sought to associate Catholics as well, in order to provide them with a "Christian" moral education, that is, a vague religiosity that could suit heretics as well as Catholics.

One of the reasons why St. Pius X condemned *Le Sillon*, Marc Sangnier's democratic movement with cultural and social aims, imbued with Modernism, was its interdenominational character (see the apostolic letter *Notre charge apostolique*, AAS 2, page 625 ff.). Among other things, the blessed pontiff wrote:

" 'All, Catholics, Protestants, and free thinkers, will have at heart to arm the youth, not for a fratricidal struggle, but for a generous emulation in the field of social and civic virtues' [Declaration by Marc Sangnier, Paris, May 1910]. These statements and this new organization of Sillonist action call for very serious reflection. Here we have an interconfessional association founded by Catholics to work for the reform of civilization, a primarily religious undertaking; for there can be no true civilization without moral civilization, and no true moral civilization without true religion: this is a proven truth, a historical fact. [...] What are we to think of an association where all religions and even free thought can express themselves openly and at ease? For the Sillonists, who proudly proclaim their individual faith in public conferences and elsewhere, certainly do not intend to silence others and prevent Protestants from affirming their Protestantism and skeptics from affirming their skepticism."[36]

— 39 —

Catholic associations that seek to provide exclusively for Catholics cultural, recreational, sporting, and other activities, with the intention of separating them from unhealthy environments, should not be commended. It is, in fact, preferable for Catholics to frequent the most varied environments in order to exercise their apostolate through infiltration and conquest.
Catholic associations that seek to provide exclusively for Catholics activities of a cultural, recreational, or sporting nature should be commended, for they contribute effectively to preserving the good from occasions of sin and provide them with excellent means of formation and sanctification. Lay people thus formed will be apostles of great value for the spread of Catholic doctrine in the various circles with which they come into contact through their daily duties.

Explanation

The rejected proposal disregards a fundamental principle of apostolate: the formation of elites for the spread of Christ's reign. However, such elites can only be formed in environments of high religious standing, which cannot be achieved without selecting the individuals who frequent them.

---

36 *Modern Doctrines*, Saint Pius X (*Lamentabili, Pascendi,* and *Letter on the Sillon*), Paris, Nouvelle Aurore, 1976, pp. 99–100.

The objection also has the disadvantage of not distinguishing between the environments that a Catholic is obliged to frequent out of duty, and those in which he voluntarily exposes himself. To illustrate the first case, let us take the example of a young person who, in order not to starve to death, is forced to accept a job in a place that is dangerous for his salvation: he will be able to count on God's special graces and will be able to resist all the better if his formation has been more thorough. In the second case, if this young person frequents dangerous places without any reason of necessity, he voluntarily exposes himself to danger and then runs the risk of seeing the words of the Holy Ghost come true for him: "*Qui amat periculum in illo peribit* — and he that loveth danger shall perish in it" (Eccl 3:27). That the incriminated maxim encourages an attitude contrary to the Tradition of the Church and the desires of the Holy See for the present times is obvious from the recommendations given by Pope Pius XII to the members of the International Catholic Association for the Protection of Girls. In an address to the members of this association gathered in Rome for a congress in September 1948, the Pope said:

"You provide moral security for young girls through reception centers, homes, hotels, boarding houses, and restaurants of impeccable reputation, through secretariats, placement and guidance services, and permanent offices in train stations and seaports and airports: this is excellent and very urgent."[37]

As we can see, the Supreme Pontiff believes that effective apostolate requires distancing oneself from the worldly environment. The people we want to be apostles to must be attracted by an atmosphere that is healthy, welcoming, and imbued with deep morality. In such a setting, religious training, the acquisition of domestic skills, the development of artistic talents, and the education of young people in practical

---

37 *Pontifical Documents of His Holiness Pius XII*, 1948, Paris, Labergerie, p. 357.

life can be achieved easily and successfully.[38]

— 40 —

Only ecclesiastical authority has the power to repress errors relating to the faith that arise among Catholics. The faithful themselves have only the right to report these errors to the local Ordinary. They are not permitted to attack these errors orally or in writing, unless the ecclesiastical authority has already taken the initiative.

A doctrine can only be officially condemned in the name of the Church by ecclesiastical authority. However, any faithful who encounters a doctrine that has already been condemned has the right and, in many cases, the duty to combat it. If they encounter a doctrine that has not yet been expressly condemned but is incompatible with the teachings of the Church, they can and, in many cases, must, under their own personal responsibility, point out such incompatibility and oppose, as far as possible, the propagation of this doctrine.

Explanation

The refuted proposition runs counter to the entire Tradition of the Church. Indeed, as a general rule, the condemnation of heresiarchs such as Luther, Jansenius, and, more recently, the Modernists, was always preceded by controversies that shed light on the issue, opposing the innovators to a few valiant defenders of the faith, both clergy and laity, acting on their own responsibility.[39]

38 See *Civiltà Cattolica*, October 16, 1948.
39 Dom Guéranger, in his famous *Liturgical Year*, on the feast of St. Cyril of Alexandria (February 9), gave a commentary that illustrates this truth: "When the shepherd turns into a wolf, it is up to the flock to defend itself first. Regularly, no doubt, doctrine descends from the bishops to the faithful, and the subjects, in matters of faith, have no right to judge their leaders. But there are essential points in the treasure of Revelation which every Christian, by virtue of his title of Christian, has the necessary knowledge of and is obliged to guard."

However, it is always meritorious to inform the ecclesiastical authority, which can only look favorably upon this struggle undertaken by the faithful against error, in justice and charity.

IV— On the Spiritual Life

— 41 —

Union with God consists in vital and experiential contact with Christ; moral union, that is, the exercise of the virtues, is incidental to this end.

It is not possible to distinguish between God's essence and his holiness. Hence the falsity of any conception that claims, formally or implicitly, that union with the divine essence is possible without at the same time there being union with the holiness of God. Consequently, the separation that some claim to make between ontological union and moral union (through obedience to the commandments) is equally false, since both result from sanctifying grace, infused virtues, and actual graces. As for grace and its operations, they are in themselves beyond the realm of experience (cf. I-II, q. 112, a. 5; *De Veritate* q. 10, a. 10).

Explanation

The refuted proposition has a strongly modernist character, in that it consists mainly, if not exclusively, of spiritual life as an ontological and experiential union with God, placing itself on a field that is outside the operation of the faculties of the soul, a field that is, so to speak, transpsychological.

In the moral order, this leads to laxity. If union with God is not achieved through union with divine holiness, all the commandments become incidental or superfluous, since they do not lead to the ultimate end, which is God. It is as if two forms of spirituality were being instituted: one for those who fly toward the wide expanses of ontological and experiential union with God, the other for those who, under the guidance of moralists, crawl on the earth, practicing the commandments.

Union with God stems above all from participation in the divine nature, which is achieved through sanctifying grace. But it is not independent of the fulfillment of the commandments, without which it cannot subsist or develop. St. Thomas affirms (I-II, q. 4, a. 4, c.):

"Rectitudo voluntatis requiritur ad beatitudinem et antecedenter et concomitanter. Antecedenter quidem, quia rectitudo voluntatis est per debitum ordinem ad finem ultimum. Finis autem comparatur ad id quod ordinatur ad finem, sicut forma ad materiam. Unde sicut materia non po test consequi formam, nisi sit debito modo disposita ad ipsam, ita nilil consequitur finem, nisi sit debito modo ordinatum ad ipsum. Et idco nullus potest ad beatitudinem pervenire, nisi habeat rectitudinem volun tatis. Concomitanter autem, quia, sicut dictum est, beatitudo ultima consistit in visione divinæ essentiæ, quæ est ipsa essentia bonitatis. Et ila volontas videntis Dei essentiam, ex necessitate amat quidquid amat, sub ordine ad Deum. »

"The rectitude of the will is required for beatitude, both as a precondition and as a concomitant. As a precondition, because what makes the will rectitude is its proper relation to the ultimate end. Now the end, with regard to what is ordered to it, plays the same role as form with regard to matter. Just as matter cannot obtain form unless it is suitably disposed, so nothing can attain its end unless it is in a right relationship to it. And that is why no one can attain beatitude unless they have a right will. This rightness is also required by concomitance; for, as we have said, supreme beatitude consists in the vision of the divine essence, which is the very essence of good. And so, the will of the one who sees the essence of God necessarily loves everything it loves in reference to God."

— 42 —

For the faithful to be united with Christ, effort in the practice of virtue and the fulfillment of precepts is secondary and almost useless. To attach great importance to the practice of virtues and to recommend obedience to the commandments is reprehensible "moralism" or "virtue-centrism."

Effort in the practice of virtue and the fulfillment of precepts is indispensable for the faithful to obtain, preserve, and increase union with Christ, the fruit of sanctifying grace. Attachment to the practice of the commandments is legitimate and necessary, as long as this concern does not turn into obsession.

Explanation

Given human weakness, man is easily inclined to value what elevates him — sanctifying grace — without looking at what imposes obligations on him — moral law. It is understandable that the Church, like a good mother, insists on what is most difficult, namely the practice of the commandments. There is no possibility of reprehensible "moralism" in this. Such was the attitude of the divine founder of the Church, Jesus Christ. What would be reprehensible would be to give into the exaggerations of Pelagianism: to conceive the act of virtue as purely natural, independent of grace and capable of obtaining union with God by itself.

— 43 —

"Moralism" or "virtue-centrism" fixes the believer's attention on himself, diverting it from God. Man, preoccupied with his moral problems, tends to become the center of his spiritual life. This is the hideous "anthropocentrism" diametrically opposed to true Catholic piety, which is "theocentric."

> When the faithful turn to themselves to combat a fault or acquire a virtue, they perform an excellent act, ordered to union with God, provided they do so for a supernatural motive. There is nothing "anthropocentric" about this, since man turns to himself only to better unite himself with God. For, according to scholastic doctrine, what is first in intention is last in execution.

Explanation

Since the rectitude of the will is a necessary means of approaching God, everything that Christians do for their progress in virtue and moral perfection has God himself, and not simply man, as its center and measure. All Christian asceticism is therefore necessarily theocentric.

Moreover, the refuted proposition is not a new error. Already, among the propositions of Miguel de Molinos condemned by Innocent XI (November 20, 1687), the ninth, in particular, targeted this same attitude applied to one's own faults (DS 2209 42).[40] And recently, Pope Pius XII devoted several pages of *Mediator Dei* (AAS 39, pages 533 to 537) to condemning this false conception of asceticism, shared by many Catholics who claim to suppress the effort to overcome passions and be united with Christ.

---

40 Quietist error #9: "The soul must remember neither itself nor God nor anything else, and in the interior way all reflection is harmful, even reflection on one's human actions and one's own faults."

— 44 —

The spirituality of the Exercises of St. Ignatius and, in general, the schools of spirituality born under the influence of the Counter-Reformation, such as those of St. John of the Cross, St. Alphonsus Liguori, etc., are imbued with "anthropocentrism," "virtue-centrism," and "moralism." They were useful as reactions against Protestantism, but they have no permanent value because they diverted Christian piety from the authentic "theocentric" path.

The schools of spirituality that emerged after the Protestant Reformation, like all those approved by the Church, although they differ from one another in ways that can be explained by the freedom with which the Holy Ghost instructs and guides the saints, are fundamentally all "theocentric" and remain effective for all time, as demonstrated by the Holy See's repeated recommendations, even today, of the Spiritual Exercises of St. Ignatius and, in general, of schools of spirituality.[41]

Explanation

It is so essential to all spirituality to be "theocentric" that the slightest deviation on this point constitutes a very serious error. It is incomprehensible how the Church, which is infallible in all matters relating to the edification of the faithful, could have approved methods that lead away from God, or how the faithful could have attained heroic virtue by following these methods. The refuted proposition implicitly casts doubt on the infallibility of the Church.

---

41 See, in addition to *Mens Nostra* by Pius XI on the Spiritual Exercises of St. Ignatius, *Mediator Dei*, AAS 39, pp. 585 and 586.

— 45 —

A spirituality that places great emphasis on meditation and, in general, on practices of piety through which the individual exercises his faculties to inspire good intentions in himself, is based on secondary, even imperfect, means of sanctification. Only liturgical practices, by virtue of their *ex opere operato* action, ensure the full development of the spiritual life and union with God.

According to *Mediator Dei*, the intensity of the faithful's participation in liturgical acts is conditioned by their interior dispositions. Meditation, examination of conscience, and other similar practices have always been recommended by the Church as indispensable means of acquiring such dispositions. It would also be rash to despise private prayer as a means of achieving the same goal. Consequently, participation in liturgical acts, private prayer, meditation, and other similar practices complement each other, and the faithful should not choose between one or the other, but use them all.

Explanation

The refuted proposition would be true if, for an adult, sanctification *ex opere operato*, which dispenses with the need for interior dispositions, were possible. But *Mediator Dei* links "objective" or liturgical piety to "subjective" or private piety, showing that both are legitimate and that one cannot do without the other (4AS 39, page 532 ff.).

Furthermore, specifically for Brazil, the Sacred Congregation for Seminaries teaches the following:

"Renunciation of oneself, of one's own ways of seeing things, of the desire to dominate and be admired, can only be acquired through prayer, through meditation on the life of Jesus and the words he spoke for all generations, and through patient practice, controlled by frequent examinations of conscience. Without victory in this area of spiritual combat, it is not possible to attain the Christian humility required to be totally submissive to God's will (AAS 42, page 843)."

— 46 —

It is characteristic of Catholic Action, the official apostolate of the Church, to have a spirituality nourished exclusively by liturgical practices, which are the expression of official piety. On the other hand, it is up to religious associations — Apostleship of Prayer, pious unions, etc. — which are purely private apostolic works, to cultivate extra-liturgical piety.

The obligation to devote oneself to liturgical and extra-liturgical piety is common to all the faithful, without distinction, whatever association they belong to.

Explanation

As we said above, Pope Pius XII, in *Mediator Dei*, emphatically declares that the two forms of piety are complementary and indispensable.

— 47 —

Devotion to the saints, and especially to Our Lady, easily distracts the faithful from true Catholic piety, which is, par excellence, "Christocentric."

Devotion to the saints, and especially to the Blessed Virgin, in no way leads the faithful away from Jesus Christ. On the contrary, it is an excellent, normal, and, in the case of the Blessed Virgin, necessary way to achieve union with Jesus Christ.

Explanation

Religious ignorance and certain pagan superstitions lead many people to make saints the object of false piety, an abuse which, moreover, also exists with regard to Christ. This is sometimes seen in certain regions of our diocese or in other parts of Brazil. The risk does not lie, strictly speaking, in devotion to the saints, but in religious ignorance and, above all, in superstitions inherited from pagan ancestors. Devotion to the saints and to Our Lady, as it exists among most pious people in our cities, shows no signs of exaggeration or anything that might give rise to fears that such abuses might occur. Moreover, according to St. Thomas (IV Sent. d. 45, q. 3, a. 2), our prayers must rise to the throne of God through the same channel through which divine blessings descend; and since these blessings have taken the path of intercession by the saints, it is through devotion to the saints that we approach God.

On the role and necessity of Mary in our sanctification, St. Pius X wrote:

"All of us, therefore, who are united with Christ, are, as the Apostle says, members of his body, born of his flesh and bones [Eph 5:10], and we must say that we originate from the womb of the Virgin, from which we came forth one day like a body attached to its head."

And further on:

"If, then, the Blessed Virgin is both Mother of God and Mother of men, who can doubt that she uses all her powers with her Son, the head of the body of the Church [Col 1:18], so that he may pour out upon us, who are his members, the gifts of his grace, especially that of knowing him and living through him [1 Jn 4:9]. [...] Mary, as St. Bernard rightly observes, is the aqueduct [Sermon for the Nativity of the Virgin "De aquæductu," no. 4] or, if you will, the neck that connects the body to the head and through which the head exercises its power and influence over the body. (Encyclical *Ad diem illum*, February 2, 1904.)"[42]

---

42 See *Pontifical Documents of His Holiness St. Pius X*, vol. I (1903-1908), Versailles, Publications du Courrier de Rome, 1993, p. 98.

– 48 –

> Assiduous attendance at the sacrament of penance is an excess of devotion that should be condemned. The Church asks the faithful to receive this sacrament only once a year. The *Confiteor* recited at the foot of the altar when participating in Holy Mass is sufficient to obtain forgiveness of sins.

> **Assiduous attendance at the sacrament of penance is encouraged by the Church and recommended by all doctors of spiritual life. The *Confiteor* of the Mass cannot remit mortal sins. As for the forgiveness of venial sins, if one has contrition and the intention to correct oneself, it can be obtained through sacramentals, such as the *Confiteor* of the Mass. A person who renounces the practice of frequent confession in order to use only sacramentals would be depriving themselves of the benefits and graces that only the sacrament of penance confers, and would be acting in contradiction to the thinking of the Holy Church.**

Explanation

The refuted proposition supports an ascetic opinion condemned by the Tradition of the Church and recently proscribed by Pius XII in *Mystici Corporis Christi* on June 29, 1943, in the following words:

"This is also the result of the erroneous doctrine that frequent confession of venial sins should not be given so much importance, since it is inferior in value to the general confession that the Bride of Christ, together with her children who are united to her in the Lord, makes every day through her priests before ascending the altar. [DS 3818.]"

And further on, he insists:

"In order to advance with increasing zeal on the path of virtue, We strongly recommend this pious practice, introduced by the Church under the inspiration of the Holy Ghost, of frequent confession, which increases true self-knowledge, promotes Christian humility, tends to uproot bad habits, combats spiritual negligence and lukewarmness, purifies the conscience, strengthens the will, lends itself to spiritual direction, and, through the specific effect of the sacrament, increases grace. [DS 3818.]"

He concludes with this painful warning:

"Therefore, those who despise and cause the ecclesiastical youth to lose esteem for frequent confession should know that they are doing something contrary to the Spirit of Christ and very harmful to the Mystical Body of the Savior. [AAS 35, page 235.]"

— 49 —

The orders of superiors must be obeyed insofar as they appear relevant to inferiors. Obeying imprudent orders denotes a servility incompatible with Christian dignity.
Christian obedience consists in submitting to all orders issued by legitimate superiors, provided that they do not lead to sin, because of the good that comes from obeying superiors. Inferiors do not have the power to disobey an order simply because they do not consider it prudent.

Explanation

The refuted proposition destroys the entire foundation of authority by basing it on the consent of subjects, an error prohibited in the condemnation of Liberalism. Catholic doctrine, on the contrary, teaches that authority comes from God and that, for this reason, it must be obeyed even when the orders it gives seem incomprehensible or imprudent to inferiors. It is precisely in this that obedience is a virtue, for while the refuted proposition makes obedience an act of the intellect alone, Catholic doctrine sees it first and foremost as an act of the will. And without an act of the will, there is no virtue. See, on this subject, the teaching of St. Peter (1 Peter 2:8) when he recommends obedience even to difficult superiors.

V — On the New Morality

— 50 —

In the realm of human activities (commerce, arts, literature, leisure, sports, etc.), man must consider only the principles specific to each field. Thus, a work of art, for example, will be perfect if it is artistically successful; sport will be perfect if it achieves its goals, etc. None of these fields is subordinate to general moral principles.

All the immediate ends to which human activities tend are ordered to an ultimate end that gives them unity and value. The principles that concern this ultimate end therefore also govern the secondary ends relating to each specific field of human activity.

Explanation

The refuted proposition belongs to the so-called "new" morality condemned by the Holy Father [Pius XII] in his address of March 23, 1952.[43] It denies the teleological unity of man and therefore the subordination of all his actions to an ultimate end, and consequently the subordination of all areas of human activity to a higher set of moral rules, applicable, *servatis servandis* [all things considered], to all branches of activity in which man engages.

---

43 Radio message on the occasion of "Family Day" (March 23, 1952): "[...] In Catholic morality, as in dogma, there is a desire to carry out a radical revision of sorts in order to deduce a new order of values. The first step, or rather the first blow to the edifice of Christian moral rules, should be to free it — as some claim — from the close and oppressive supervision of the Church's authority. freed from the subtleties and sophisms of casuistic method, morality would be restored to its original form and to the determination of individual conscience. [...] It is worth highlighting the cardinal vice of this "new morality." By leaving all ethical criteria to the individual conscience, jealously closed in on itself and made the absolute arbiter of its own determinations, this theory, far from smoothing the way, diverts it from the true path, which is Christ." (*Pontifical Documents of His Holiness Pius XII*, 1952, p. 85; AAS 44, p. 270 ff.)

The refuted statement logically leads to the doctrine of those who affirm the absolute identification between being and good, such that any increase in the line of being is equivalent to progress in the line of good *simpliciter* (see St. Thomas, I, q. 5, a. 1, ad 1).[44] Thus, for example, the more an artist progresses as an artist, the more he progresses in the good in absolute terms. Since God is at the summit of the line of being, those who progress along this line thereby approach God, who is the Supreme Good. According to this conception, the conformity or nonconformity of a work of art with moral precepts is extrinsic and cannot in any way affect the ontological ascent toward God.

---

44 "Good (*bonum*) and being (*ens*) may be identical in reality (*secundum rem*), but since they differ in concept (*secundum rationem*), it is not in the same way that a thing is said to be purely and simply (*ens simpliciter*) and purely and simply good (*bonum simpliciter*). [...] Indeed, it is by its substantial being (*per suum esse substantiale*) that a thing is said to be purely and simply (*ens simpliciter*), while by its superadded acts (*per actus superadditos*), it is said to be only in some respect (*esse secundum quid*). [...] Conversely, the good (*bonum*) includes the reason for perfection (*dicit rationem perfecti*), which is what we strive for, and therefore the ultimate reason. From this it follows that what is in possession of its ultimate perfection is said to be good purely and simply (*bonum simpliciter*), but what does not have the ultimate perfection that it should have, even though it has some perfection according to what it is in act, will not be said to be perfect or good purely and simply (*perfectum vel bonum simpliciter*), but only in a certain respect (*secundum quid*). [...]". In other words, it is by its primary and substantial being that a thing is *ens simpliciter*, and it is by its ultimate being or ultimate perfection that it is *bonum simpliciter*.

— 51 —

The Catholic press must treat each subject according to the principles specific to that subject, disregarding principles that are superior to each field. Thus, when it makes a moral critique of entertainment, it may censor a film because the specific object of that section is morality; but in its advertising pages, it may advertise the same film, because that section is concerned only with advertising; and so on in the other sections devoted to art, sports, etc., all of which must follow their own principles, independently of morality or religion.

Religious and moral principles must govern all sections of newspapers, especially when they have as their special purpose the propagation and defense of Catholic doctrine. The publication of immoral advertisements in Catholic press outlets is scandalous. It is also scandalous that there should be a contradiction between the page devoted to film reviews and the commercial page.

Explanation

See the explanation of the previous proposition.

— 52 —

The moral rule must be instilled as a norm that is appropriate for man by virtue of the natural order of things. And it is preferable to remain silent about its character as a precept coming from God and made obligatory by the force of divine authority manifested in Revelation. For this character of precept and obligation revolts and shocks the mentality of contemporary man.

> The essential point of moral formation lies in the recognition of God's supreme sovereignty over all men and all things. Consequently, a moral formation that claims conformity with human nature as its principal or exclusive foundation is flawed in principle and will never reach the realm of the supernatural.

Explanation

The refuted sentence is profoundly revolutionary. It capitulates to man's revolt against the authority of the Creator. This does not mean that, once the commandment has been recognized and accepted as imposed by God, it is useless to show, in order to make it easier to practice, that it corresponds in fact to the nature of man created by God and object of his love. But a moral formation based solely on this consideration, which is much less important than the first [the sovereign authority of God], would have failed radically.

When it comes to convincing non-Catholics, we can show the harmony of the Catholic religion with human nature: this is a way of smoothing the path, provided we are dealing with people whose good faith is evident. However, an apologetic demonstration that would stop there would be fundamentally insufficient. Catholicism is a religion of obedience and must be presented as such.

— 53 —

It is characteristic of traditional religious associations, such as Marian congregations, pious unions, the Children of Mary, etc., to advise their members against wearing makeup, attending dancehalls, going to public swimming pools, going on mixed outings, etc. Catholic Action, on the contrary, conceived according to the most recent moral guidelines of the Church, must authorize, promote, and encourage these practices, which allow its members to adapt to the century in which we live and thus enable them to carry out their apostolate.

The morality of the Church is immutable, and what was vanity, a source of scandal or sin yesterday, is still so today and will always be so tomorrow. Therefore, the Church will never approve of modern dances, mixed or public swimming pools, mixed sports, public displays of women's sports, etc. And she will always praise those who renounce makeup and any other sign of vanity and worldliness.

Explanation

The refuted proposal would be logical if one accepted the idea of a new morality in the Church, one that is freer and more convenient, of which Catholic Action would be the herald. But on the contrary, this organization, which has received so much encouragement to its credit and such precious blessings from the sovereign pontiffs, must consider the practice of the most rigorous principles of Christian modesty to be fully appropriate to it. The Supreme Pontiff has expressed himself in no other way in the various addresses he has given to young Catholic women, as can be seen in *Acta Apostolicæ Sedis*

35, page 142 (April 24, 1943),[45] 33, page 186 (May 22, 1941);[46]

45 Address to the young women of Italian Catholic Action (April 24, 1943): "[...] The dignity and freedom of women who never allow themselves to be enslaved, not even by fashion! This is a delicate but urgent subject, where your tireless efforts will promise happy and beneficial success. However, your zeal against immodest clothing and behavior must not only be a condemnation but also an edification, showing the female world in a practical way how a young woman can harmonize in her dress and behavior the higher laws of virtue with the norms of hygiene and elegance. It is to be hoped that a large number of Italian women, at least those who have remained sane in mind and heart, will not delay or hesitate to follow your example." (*Pontifical Documents of His Holiness Pius XII*, 1943, p. 106.)
46 Address to the young women of Catholic Action in Rome, members of the Crusade of Purity (May 22, 1941): "[...] We do not propose to retrace here the sad and all too familiar picture of the disorders that present themselves to your eyes: clothing so skimpy or such that it seems designed to highlight rather than conceal what it should veil; sports events that take place in conditions of clothing, exhibitionism, and camaraderie that are incompatible with even the most modest standards; dances, shows, auditions, readings, illustrations, ornaments, where the desire for entertainment and pleasure accumulates the most serious dangers. [...]

"In the attitude to be observed towards fashion, virtue holds the middle ground. What God asks of you is to always remember that fashion is not and cannot be the supreme rule of your conduct, that above fashion and its demands, there are higher and more imperious laws, superior and immutable principles which, under no circumstances, can be sacrificed to pleasure or whim and before which the idol of fashion must know how to bow down its fleeting power. These principles have been proclaimed by God, by the Church, by the saints, by reason, and by Christian morality. They are signals that mark the limits beyond which lilies and roses no longer bloom, or feminine purity, modesty, dignity, and honor no longer exude their fragrance, but where an unhealthy air of levity, equivocal language, audacious vanity, and fatuity reigns in the heart as well as in clothing. These are the principles that St. Thomas Aquinas sets forth and recalls concerning women's dress [*Expositio in Isaiam prophetam*, ch. III in fine], indicating what the order of our charity and affections should be: the good of our soul takes precedence over that of our body, and we must prefer the good of our neighbor's soul to the advantage of our own body (II-II, q. 169, a. 2). Therefore, do you not see that there is a limit that no form of fashion can allow to be exceeded, a limit beyond which fashion becomes a source of ruin for the soul of women and for the souls of others?

Some young women may say that a certain style of dress is more comfortable and also more hygienic; but if it becomes a serious and imminent danger to the salvation of the soul, it is certainly not hygienic for

32, page 414 (October 6, 1940).[47]

your spirit, and it is your duty to renounce it. The desire to save their souls made martyrs such as Agnes and Cecilia heroic in the midst of the torments and lacerations of their virginal bodies. You, their sisters in faith, in the love of Christ, and in the esteem of virtue, would you not find in your hearts the courage and strength to sacrifice a little comfort, a physical advantage, if you will, in order to keep your souls healthy and pure? And if no one has the right to endanger the physical life of others for the sake of mere personal pleasure, is it not even less permissible to compromise their salvation, and thus the very life of their souls? If, as some claim, daring fashion makes no bad impression on them, what do they know of the impression it makes on others? Who can assure them that others will not be badly influenced by it? You do not know the depths of human frailty, nor how corrupt the wounds left in human nature by Adam's sin are, with ignorance in the intellect, malice in the will, greed for pleasure, and weakness toward the arduous good in the passions of the senses, to such an extent that man, as pliable as wax to evil, 'sees what is better and approves of it, and clings to what is worse' [Ovid, *Metamorphoses*, VII, 20-21], because of this weight that always, like lead, drags him down. Oh! How rightly it has been observed that if certain Christian women suspected the temptations and falls they cause in others by their dress and the familiarities to which, in their light-heartedness, they attach so little importance, they would be horrified by their responsibility!" (*Pontifical Documents of His Holiness Pius XII*, 1941, pp. 128-132.)

47 Address to the young women of Catholic Action (October 6, 1940): "[...] Do you not know that your members are the sanctuary of the Holy Ghost, who dwells in you, to whom you belong on God's behalf, no longer belonging to yourselves?" (1 Cor. 6:19). The conscious awareness of this divine indwelling, of this incorporation into Christ, has given rise to and developed over the centuries among peoples docile to the Gospel a religious respect for the body that is reflected in a set of arrangements for the person, manners, demeanor, and words that are wisely regulated and measured: modesty. And from the beginning of the Church, the same apostle wanted women to wear veils in sacred gatherings and said to the Corinthians: 'You yourselves judge: doth it become a woman, to pray unto God uncovered? (...) But if a woman nourish her hair, it is a glory to her; for her hair is given to her for a covering.' (1 Cor. 11:13 and 15).

Your apostolate will act above all by example. It will be up to [...] your wise leaders to teach you how, before wearing an item of clothing, you must ask your conscience how Jesus Christ would judge it; to warn you that before accepting an invitation, you must consider whether your invisible and heavenly guardian angel will be able to follow you to such an appointment without covering his face with his wings. They will tell you which shows, which companies, which beaches you should avoid; they

On the subject of balls, Pope Pius XI, in his encyclical *Ubi arcano Dei*, stated: "No one is unaware that the frivolity of women and young girls has already exceeded the limits of modesty, especially in clothing and dancing" (AAS 14, pages 678-679). Before him, Benedict XV had already lamented the indecency of women's clothing and the lack of restraint and modesty in dancing. After lamenting the "blindness of women" and the "madness of clothing," he added the following about dances: "They have entered into the customs of society, coming from barbarism, each worse than the other, and more apt than anything else to remove all modesty" (Encyclical *Sacra prope diem*, January 6, 1921, AAS 13, page 39).

With regard to women's sporting events held in public, the Sacred Congregation of the Council promulgated an instruction on January 12, 1930, which contains the following terms "Parents should forbid (*arceant*) their daughters from participating in public exercises and gymnastics competitions; if their daughters are obliged to take part, they should ensure that they wear clothes that respect modesty and never tolerate immodest costumes" (Instruction on indecent female fashions, decision III).[48] Pope Pius XII spoke in the same vein when he addressed doctors and physical education teachers on November 8, 1952.[49]

---

will show you how a young woman can be modern, cultured, athletic, full of grace, naturalness, and distinction, without bowing to all the vulgarities of an unhealthy fashion, preserving a face that is free from artifice, like the soul it reflects, a gaze without inner or outer shadows, but at the same time reserved, sincere, and frank. For the generous and active defense of your purity, we recommend above all prayer and, in a special way, the worship of the Holy Eucharist and of the Immaculate Virgin to whom you are consecrated." (*Pontifical Documents of His Holiness Pius XII*, 1940, pp. 303-305.)

48 *Acts of Pius XI*, Bonne Presse, vol. VI, p. 353; AAS 22, p. 26.

49 Address to physical education teachers (November 8, 1952): "[...] No less important is another fundamental rule also contained in a passage from Holy Scripture. In St. Paul's letter to the Romans, we read: 'But I see another law in my members, fighting against the law of my mind, and captivating me in the law of sin, that is in my members.' (Romans 7:23). One could not describe more vividly the daily drama that is woven into human life. The

— 54 —

Low-cut necklines, swimsuits, and other such clothing that largely exposes the body should not be prohibited, for the body is good in itself, was created by God, and does not need to be hidden.

The human body was created by God and, like everything else, is good in itself. But after original sin, it was corrupted by concupiscence. For this reason, it is appropriate to cover the body so that it does not become an occasion for sin.

Explanation

The refuted statement is inspired by a viscerally anti-Catholic Naturalism.

---

instincts and forces of the body make themselves felt, stifling the voice of reason, and prevail over the energies of good will from the day their full subordination to the spirit was lost through original sin.

"In the intensive use and exercise of the body, this fact must be taken into account. Just as there are forms of gymnastics and sports which, by their austerity, help to restrain the instincts, so there are other forms of sport which awaken them, either by violent force or by the seductions of sensuality. From an aesthetic point of view, too, through the pleasure of beauty, through the admiration of rhythm in dance and gymnastics, instinct can insinuate its venom into souls. Moreover, in sports and gymnastics, in rhythmic exercises and in dance, there is a certain nudity that is neither necessary nor appropriate. It is not without reason that a few decades ago a completely impartial observer admitted: 'What interests the masses in this area is not the beauty of nudity, but the nudity of beauty.' Religious and moral sensibilities oppose this way of practicing gymnastics and sport. In short, sport and gymnastics should not command and dominate, but serve and help. That is their function, and that is where they find their justification." (*Pontifical Documents of His Holiness Pius XII*, 1952, pp. 516-517 or EPS, *Le Corps humain*, Desclée, 1953, 401-402.)

— 55 —

We must not criticize people who come to receive Communion wearing makeup, low-cut tops, short sleeves, or bare legs. It would be a lack of charity to refuse them the sacraments, since these people do not do so maliciously (if that were the case, they would not come to church dressed that way). Furthermore, to see malice in everything is to blame God himself, the creator of the human body.

The Church advises against makeup and prohibits low-cut necklines, sleeveless garments, bare legs, etc. The faithful must be instructed in the doctrine of the Catholic Church on this point, because after original sin, the human body became a slave to concupiscence, and any imprudence in this matter is dangerous, to say the least.

Explanation

The human body is good in itself, like all of God's creatures. The obligation for humans not to expose it does not come from the human body as God created it, but from the disorder of instincts resulting from original sin.

This is why the Church recommends great modesty in dress.

The feeling of shame caused by the immodest display of the human body cannot be called malice, but modesty. For distinguishing between good and evil, far from being a defect, is, on the contrary, the foundation of all virtues. Therefore, to rebuke those who dress immodestly is to excite in them, not malice, but virtue.

This is why Church law obliges priests to refuse the sacraments to people who present themselves immodestly (Sacred Congregation of the Council, January 12, 1930, decision no. 9, AAS 22, pages 26 and 27).[50]

The refuted proposition considers the question as if humanity

---

50 "Young girls and women who dress immodestly should be forbidden access to the holy table, the role of godmother at baptism and confirmation, and, if circumstances warrant, even entry into the Church."

were not in a state of fallen nature. Furthermore, it denies the existence of objective good and evil: in concrete cases, it would not be found in an objective fact — the immodesty of clothing or the transgression of the precept that prohibits immodest clothing — but rather in the subjective state of mind of the one who sees immorality in nudity.

A concrete application will show the extent to which the refuted sentence is opposed to the true spirit of the Church. The saints have always distinguished themselves by their extreme sensitivity in perceiving and rejecting anything that even remotely opposes angelic virtue. While the Church sees this as a refinement of modesty, for the proponents of the erroneous proposition, it would be a refinement of malice!

On the subject of feminine vanity, St. Paul (1 Tim. 2:9) and St. Peter (1 Peter 3:5) give valuable recommendations. See also Isaiah, chapter III, verses 16 to 24.

— 56 —

It is useful for members of Catholic Action to participate in carnival celebrations in order to carry out their apostolate. That being said, spiritual retreats, which separate them from the world, should not be held for members of Catholic Action during the days of carnival.

It is illicit to put oneself in an occasion of sin under the pretext of apostolate. Since carnival celebrations are an occasion of sin, the faithful must abstain from them.

Explanation

The Brazilian carnival is infamous throughout the world for the immoralities to which it gives rise, and everything indicates that it is going from bad to worse.[51] The participation of the faithful in these immoral amusements is not only a danger to their souls, but also a serious scandal to their neighbors. On the other hand, isolating oneself in contemplation and prayer

51 This text dates from 1953. What can we say today!

during these three days causes no small edification and is, in itself, an excellent form of apostolate.

The erroneous proposition seems to ignore the existence of proximate occasions of sin, at least for those who claim to be apostles. Let us therefore recall the condemnation issued by Innocent XI against moral laxity (March 2, 1679), which advocated, among other things, the following postulates: "It is permissible to seek out the proximate occasion of sin for our spiritual or temporal good or for that of our neighbor" (proposition 63); "A proximate occasion of sin should not be avoided when there is a useful or honest reason not to avoid it" (proposition 62; DS2163 and 2162).

– 57 –

Divorced persons who remarry may be admitted to participate publicly in campaigns to collect funds for spiritual or material works of mercy.
It is lawful to receive alms from public sinners. But it is scandalous to introduce them into committees responsible for collecting donations for pious works, because this cannot be done without exposing them in Christian society.[52]

Explanation

The refuted proposition implicitly denies the moral unity of man, since it seems to postulate the possible coexistence of two entirely foreign aspects in the same person: in domestic life, one could be a public sinner and incur all the reprobation that this state deserves, while in public or social life, as a politician, businessman, or "philanthropist," one could continue to enjoy general respect. And the Church, turning a blind eye to one of the two sides of this life, would hold up the other as commendable. Such a way of assessing an

---

52 Obviously, the principles set forth here apply to all Catholic activities and works.

individual's behavior is erroneous, as the commentary on paragraph 50 has shown.

— 58 —

Since sexual union is a reflection of the relationships that exist in the intimate life of the Holy Trinity, it is reasonable and useful to use erotic themes to stimulate piety.

Although all honest acts performed with right intention are meritorious before God, sexual relations, in the present economy of fallen nature, are so deeply connected with unruly concupiscence that they cannot normally serve to excite or elevate piety.

Explanation

Sensual-Mystic literature is one of the scourges of our time. Pope Pius XII warned the faithful about it several times. During the previous pontificate, in an instruction dated May 3, 1927, the Sacred Congregation of the Holy Office took special measures against such writings (AAS 19, page 186 ff.).[53] One of the serious drawbacks of this literature is that it lends itself easily to expressions that lead to pantheistic mysticism. To claim to nourish piety with mystical-sensual considerations is to go against the Tradition of the Church, which has always strived to instill in the faithful, whatever their state of life, the spirit of purity by which man prepares himself for the heavenly dwelling, where *neque nubent neque nubentur* ("men have no wives and women have no husbands," Mt 22:30).

The Song of Songs has been cited, not without blasphemy,

53 Instruction on Sensual and Sensual-Mystical Literature (May 3, 1927): "Among the most disastrous evils that today totally corrupt Christian morality and cause immense harm to souls redeemed by the precious blood of Jesus Christ, we must especially condemn this kind of literature that leads to sensuality, evil passions, and a kind of lascivious mysticism. There are writers, abominably, who do not fear to pass off the nourishment of a morbid sensuality under the guise of sacred things, combining immodest love with a kind of piety toward God and with an absolutely false religious mysticism..." (*Acts of Pius XI*, vol. IV, p. 189 ff.)

in favor of Sensual-Mystical literature. The Church, the sole authentic interpreter of Sacred Scripture, has always condemned the erotic interpretation of this poem. It is certain, in fact, that the expressions found therein do not allude to the animal life of man. Nevertheless, since the loving union of the soul with God is described in a fairly realistic manner, even among the Jews, reading it was only permitted after the age of 30. Such is the prudence required in this matter.

— 59 —

The preparation of adolescents for marriage must be done in a modern way, that is, before large audiences, using realistic, lively language that is lighthearted and even humorous. Above all, the arguments must refer to nature. It is necessary not to attack men's tendency toward sentimentality, but rather to sympathize with it.

In preparing adolescents for marriage, we must above all take into account the dire consequences of original sin, which at this age make this subject especially dangerous. That is why we must take great care to impress upon them the importance of supernatural means and always avoid giving the subject inappropriate publicity, that is, publicity that is contrary to the restraint with which these issues must be addressed.

Explanation

In his address to fathers on September 18, 1951, Pope Pius XII condemned the way in which many Catholic writers treat this subject without the discretion that it requires;[54] and he urged the same precautions already prescribed by Pius XI in the encyclical *Divini illius Magistri* (AAS 22, page 49 ff.). This encyclical was supplemented by the response given by

54 Address to a group of fathers from France (September 18, 1951) "There is one area in which the education of public opinion and its correction are urgently needed. In this area, it has been perverted by propaganda that we would not hesitate to call disastrous, even though it comes from

the Sacred Congregation of the Holy Office on March 21, 1931 (AAS 23, page 118), to a consultation on education and sexual initiation. We believe it useful to transcribe here the recommendations of the Sacred Congregation:

"It is absolutely necessary, in the education of youth, to follow the method hitherto employed by the Church and by men of virtue, and recommended by the Holy Father in the encyclical on the Christian education of youth dated December 31, 1929; namely: it is necessary to ensure, first and foremost, that young people of both sexes receive a complete, firm, and uninterrupted religious education; it is necessary

---

a Catholic source and is aimed at Catholics, even if those who practice it do not seem to suspect that they are, without their knowledge, deluded by the spirit of evil. We are referring here to writings, books, and articles on sexual initiation, which are often hugely successful in bookstores today and flood the entire world, invading childhood, overwhelming the younger generation, and disturbing engaged couples and young spouses.

"[...] One is appalled by the intolerable effrontery of such literature, when even Paganism seemed to stop respectfully before the secret of marital intimacy, only to see its mystery violated and its sensual and lived vision fed to the general public and to young people. One really wonders whether the boundary is still sufficiently marked between this so-called Catholic initiation and the erotic and obscene press or illustrations, which deliberately aim to corrupt or shamefully exploit, for base interests, the basest instincts of fallen nature.

"[...] Secondly, this literature, to call it that, seems to take no account of the general experience of yesterday, today, and always, because it is based on nature, which attests that, in moral education, neither initiation instruction are of any benefit in themselves, but are, on the contrary, seriously unhealthy and harmful if they are not linked to constant discipline, vigorous self-control, and, above all, the use of the supernatural powers of prayer and the sacraments. All Catholic educators worthy of their name and their mission are well aware of the preponderant role of supernatural energies in the sanctification of man, whether young or adult, single or married. Of this, in these writings, hardly a word is breathed, if it is not passed over in silence altogether. The very principles that our predecessor, Pius XI, so wisely highlighted in his encyclical *Divini illius Magistri* concerning sex education and related issues are — sad sign of the times! — dismissed with a wave of the hand or a smile: Pius XI, they say, wrote that twenty years ago, for his time. Since then, we have come a long way!" (*Pontifical Documents of His Holiness Pius XII*, 1951, pp. 388-390.)

to inspire in young people an esteem, a desire, and a love for angelic virtue; and, above all, to instill in them constancy in prayer, assiduity in the sacraments of penance and the Holy Eucharist, and a continual and filial devotion to the Blessed Virgin Mary, Mother of Holy Purity, consecrating themselves totally to her protection; finally, that they carefully avoid dangerous reading, obscene spectacles, evil conversations, and all other occasions of sin."

And after giving this advice on how sex education should be carried out, the Sacred Congregation censures books that defend the new method of education in this area, including some written by Catholic authors.

That this ordinance of the Holy See was kept in oblivion — *more jansenistarum,* according to the custom of the Jansenists — is evident from the singularly energetic manner in which Pope Pius XII speaks of these Catholic authors in the address to fathers of families quoted above. It is useful to read this address, which appeared in the January 13, 1952, issue of *Catolicismo.*[55]

— 60 —

By Providence, the vast majority of people are called to live in the state of marriage. Schoolgirls who fall in love are therefore following a natural inclination. They should not be prevented from doing so.

---

55 *Catolicismo* was the official diocesan bulletin of Bishop de Castro Mayer in Campos. The relevant excerpts from Pius XII's speech mentioned here are quoted in the previous note.

> When it comes to choosing a state of life, educators should act as follows: 1) instruct and help students to make a choice in accordance with God's will; 2) prevent the school environment from hindering vocations that require greater generosity, namely the priesthood or religious life. Consequently, premature love or love that is not with a view to marriage must be vigorously combated, for it is pure sensuality, just as contrary to the priestly or religious vocation as it is to Christian preparation for marriage.

Explanation

Although men naturally gravitate toward the married state, it is necessary to recognize the personal vocation of each adolescent. The refuted proposal seems to consider the school environment as intended to prepare all students indiscriminately for the married state, without taking into account special vocations: the priesthood or religious life.

Furthermore, it is ambiguous because it does not distinguish between love that will gradually lead to marriage and "flirting" that seeks only carnal pleasure.

The ambiguity of the erroneous proposal also stems from the fact that it does not distinguish between falling in love at an early age and falling in love at an appropriate age. Such ambiguity is all the more dangerous because the word "love" [*namoro*] lends itself to a wide variety of interpretations.

Finally, the refuted sentence ignores original sin and considers that everything natural is good in itself: a proposition that can only be accepted on condition that this dogma is denied.

With all its ambiguity and inaccuracy, this false maxim encourages sensuality and indiscipline in schools.

VI— On Rationalism, Evolutionism, Secularism

— 61 —

Philosophy and science have their own object and method independent of sacred theology, so that the faithful, in their philosophical and scientific research, do not need to take supernatural revelation into account.
Philosophy and science have their own purpose and autonomous method. However, divine Revelation is infallible and human reason is fallible. That is why, in their studies and research, scientists and philosophers must take the teachings of the Church—the authentic interpreter of Revelation—as a criterion of certainty and as a guide, at least in a negative sense.

Explanation

There can be no disagreement between reason and faith. When there appears to be incompatibility, it is because the teaching of the faith has not been formulated with sufficient objective precision or, more likely, because reason has been mistaken in its research. But philosophers and scientists, when faced with an infallible teaching of the Church, must always reject the conclusions of their philosophy or science that conflict with that teaching.

Pope Pius XII, in his encyclical *Humani generis*, recalls the traditional doctrine in these terms:

"It is necessary to be very cautious when dealing with hypotheses—even if they have some scientific basis— that touch on the doctrine contained in Holy Scripture and Tradition. But if such conjectural opinions directly or indirectly contradict the doctrine revealed by God, such a request [namely, that the Catholic religion take them into account] could in no way be accepted (DS 3895; AAS 42, page

575).

— 62 —

It is offensive to the Church to want to admit, today, the existence of veiled heresies or the threat of declared heresy. Indeed, in its current state of development, the Church has definitively overcome these dangers.

Until the end of time, men will be tempted to sin against all virtues and therefore also against the faith. Heresy is not a disgrace to the Church, but only to heretics. So even if sacred theology has achieved a certain perfection in expressing and explaining revealed truths, and has brought real progress to the Church, this does not prevent there being individuals who rebel against the Church's teaching authority.

Explanation

See the *Pastoral Letter* [reproduced at the beginning of this book].

— 63 —

History does not provide knowledge of facts in their objective reality, but only an image of them, subjectively reconstructed by the historian.

The purpose of history is the objective reconstruction of the past. The method of historical research is intended to preserve such a reconstruction from the distortions that the subjectivity of the historian might impose on it.

Explanation

The refuted proposition destroys the foundations of the Catholic religion, which is entirely based on the historical fact of Revelation, known and transmitted in its objective reality. It was on the same principle that the Modernists relied to propagate their errors, which, in the final analysis, reduced religion to pure subjectivism.

— 64 —

Over the last few centuries, civil society has evolved in its customs and in its political, social, and economic organization toward greater simplicity and equality, in accordance with the principles of the Gospel. The Church, in turn, must follow this evolution and adopt an egalitarian organization, discipline, liturgy, and simple and democratic customs — particularly with regard to the conduct of members of the hierarchy.

Over the last few centuries, the spirit of revolution has produced continual upheavals, in the hope of destroying legitimate powers and weakening authority, whether political, social, or economic, with the aim of leveling all legitimate inequalities. The Church opposes and will continue to oppose this historical process. In the 19th century and the early decades of the 20th century, it fought against anarchistic Liberalism; in the second half of the 20th century, it is prepared to fight "with the greatest energy" against Socialism, which seriously endangers human dignity and the eternal salvation of souls (Pius XII, *Radio message to Catholics in Vienna*).[56] This is why it edifies the world through its hierarchical organization, which is of divine institution and therefore immutable, and this is also why, in its liturgy, discipline, etc., it manifests a spirit of hierarchy opposed to the revolutionary spirit.

Explanation

---

56 See *Catolicismo* no. 24, December 1952. Unfortunately, this battle did not take place; in fact, the opposite happened. The Second Vatican Council refused to condemn Communism, and the "Conciliar Church" entered into an adulterous union with the ideas of the world and the Revolution, producing the bastard fruits we know today: religious liberty, ecumenism, liturgical reform, collegiality, the new Code of Canon Law, etc.

The refuted sentence accepts as legitimate the successive revolutions of a leveling nature—Protestantism, the French Revolution, Communism—which, under the pressure of the spirit of pride and sensuality, have succeeded in transforming the earth (Leo XIII, encyclical letter *Raggiunto il 25° anno*). To want to conform the Church to a civil society modeled on this spirit is to ask the Catholic religion to capitulate. Moreover, it is to forget that the organization of the Church, in its elements that are of divine institution, is immutable.

— 65 —

Catholics must be men of their time and, as such, they must sincerely accept, without reservation, the transformations and progress that differentiate our century from previous centuries.
Catholics must be men of their time and, as such, they must sincerely accept the transformations and progress that differentiate our century from previous centuries, provided that these transformations and progress are in accordance with the spirit and doctrine of the Church and that they encourage a truly Christian civilization.

Explanation

The refuted proposition is one-sided. In every period of history, Catholics have a double duty: a duty to adapt and a duty to resist. The censured maxim considers only adaptation.

This dual duty is easy to understand. There has never been a time when all laws, institutions, customs, ways of seeing and thinking deserved only praise or only blame. On the contrary, in the best of times as in the worst, there have always been good and bad things. When faced with good, whatever it may be, our attitude can only be that advised by the Apostle: Test everything and take what is good. When faced with evil, we must also obey the Apostle's advice: "be not conformed to this world" (Romans 12:2).

However, it is important to apply both pieces of advice intelligently. It is excellent to examine all things and keep only what is good. But we must bear in mind that what is good must be in accordance not only with the letter but also with the spirit: what is good is not that which promotes both virtue and vice, but only that which always and solely promotes virtue. Therefore, when a custom, in itself irreproachable, produces an atmosphere favorable to evil, prudence dictates that it be rejected. When a law, beneficial to the one true Church, at the same time encourages heresy or unbelief, it must be fought.

Resistance to the present age must also be exercised with prudence, that is, without falling short of or going beyond its goal. We have an example of unreasonable opposition to the world, through attachment to contingent and insignificant provisions, in the return to the "table-shaped altar." This is an unjustified protest that goes far beyond the stated goal, which is the defense of the faith.[57] Furthermore, resistance to the world must not fall short of its objective. It cannot be satisfied with pure theory, without application to concrete circumstances, nor can it be content with platonic protests. It is certainly useful to teach doctrine, but it is also necessary to know the living and changing reality of concrete facts and to organize action in order to be able to intervene effectively in the course of events.

Finally, it is necessary to remember that we cannot divide the characteristics of an era into good and bad elements that are independent of each other. Every era has its own mentality, which results from both good and bad aspects. If the former prevail and the latter concern only secondary matters, the era, without being the best, can be called good. If, on the contrary, the bad elements predominate and the good is found only in a

---

57 The criticism is directed at those who, in the 1950s, insisted on a return to the supposed forms of the ancient altar. This Archeologism, which "resisted the present age" (that is, in this case, the custom of traditional altars), had nothing to do with the defense of the faith, but concealed a desire for a total upheaval of the liturgy. In fact, rather than "resistance" to the age, it was more a form of subversive "*aggiornamento*."

few details, the era must be described as bad. In the problems of the Catholic's relationship with his time, it is not enough for him to focus on accidental aspects of the world in which he lives. He must consider the general character of his time, its profound moral unity, and make up his mind on that basis. It is above all by virtue of this principle that the offending proposition must be rejected. For it does not speak to us of accepting this or that aspect of the contemporary world, but rather what constitutes its overall unity.

In the Syllabus, Pius IX condemned the following proposition: "The Roman Pontiff can and must reconcile himself and come to terms with Liberalism and modern culture" (Proposition 80 DS 2980). Obviously, this condemnation would be incomprehensible if it did not imply that progress and modern civilization in Pius IX's time, while offering some good things, were infected as a whole by the errors of the moment and especially by the Liberalism that Proposition 80 specifically mentions. Indeed, this proposition is taken from the *Jamdudum* address of March 18, 1861, in which the Sovereign Pontiff painted an impressive picture of the struggle between two irreconcilable forces, one fighting for the so-called modern civilization— "a system invented to weaken and, no doubt, do away with the Church of Christ" — the other defending the eternal principles of Christian civilization. If by modern civilization we mean what Pius IX declared, that is, a Pagan civilization being built on the ruins of the ancient Christian civilization, then the condemnation of Proposition 80 is perfectly understandable.

But what is the dominant feature of the age in which we live? Let us consult the popes. Pius XI tells us:

"As the centuries pass, from one upheaval to another, we arrive at the present revolution, which we can already say is raging on all sides and seriously threatening, with a magnitude and violence that surpass all the trials of previous persecutions against the Church. Entire peoples are in danger of falling back into a barbarism worse than that in which most of the world still found itself at the coming of the Redeemer." (*Divini Redemptoris.*)

Pius XII, in a speech on October 12, 1952, to the Union of Men of Italian Catholic Action, is no less explicit:

"Today it is not only the Eternal City and Italy that are threatened, but the whole world. Oh! Do not ask us who the 'enemy' is, or what form he takes. He is everywhere and among everyone: he knows how to be violent and cunning. Over the last few centuries, he has attempted to bring about the intellectual, moral, and social disintegration of the unity that existed in the mysterious organism of Christ. He has wanted nature without grace, reason without faith, freedom without authority, and, at times, authority without freedom. It is an "enemy" that is becoming increasingly concrete, with a surprising lack of scruples: this "enemy" has strived to make Christ a stranger in universities, in schools, in families, in the administration of justice and in legislative activity, in the assemblies of nations, where decisions about peace or war are made. Currently, he is corrupting the world through a press and entertainment that kill modesty in young men and women and destroy love between spouses; he instills a Nationalism that leads to war." (See *Catolicismo*, No. 25, January 1953.)

We will conclude as follows:

Catholics today must carefully distinguish between good and evil, support and promote all that is good, and fearlessly oppose all that is evil; in particular, they must know how to use technological progress to better exercise their apostolate.

They must take a stand against the erroneous principles that have a preponderant influence in all areas of modern life; this must be their principal apostolate.

VII – On the Relationship Between the Church and the State

– 66 –

At the present stage of human society's evolution, the state has become more aware of its own autonomy, so that it is no longer possible for it to maintain such close relations with the Church as it once did. The old "pharisaical" Christian state must be replaced in the future Christendom by a "vitally" Christian state, that is, one animated by the spirit of the Gospel, the fruit of collaboration among all Christian religions, whatever the richness of each one's message, but without the government exercising special protection toward any one of them.

The state has as its proper end the provision of temporal goods, and in this sphere it is sovereign. The Church, guardian of natural law throughout the world, has the right to impose respect for its laws and doctrines on the temporal powers. The state must declare itself officially Catholic and must put all its resources at the service of the preservation and expansion of the faith.

Explanation

The refuted sentence logically leads to the doctrine of the separation of Church and State, condemned by the Syllabus (proposition 55)[58] , and again proscribed by Leo XIII in the encyclical *Immortale Dei,* by St. Pius X in *Vehementer*, and more recently by the letter of the Sacred Congregation of Seminaries to the Brazilian episcopate (AAS 42, page 841).[59]

58 Condemned proposition: "The Church ought to be separated from the State, and the State from the Church." (DS 2955).

59 Letter from the Sacred Congregation for Seminaries to the Brazilian episcopate (March 7, 1950): "Another error, also condemned by the Church, must be avoided by Christians: Liberalism. It denies that the Church, because of its very noble purpose and divine mission, has a natural supremacy over the State. It admits and encourages the separation between

Furthermore, the refuted proposition contains several other unacceptable ideas. Strictly speaking, it amounts to saying that the union between Church and State, as it existed in the Middle Ages, was a preliminary or intermediate phase, which peoples, driven by the immanent force of evolution, would subsequently pass through. However, the Church does not accept evolutionary historical determinism, which implies the denial of free will and divine Providence. Similarly, it does not accept that the situations through which humanity has passed have supplanted a system of relations logically deduced from Revelation and the natural and immutable order of things.[60]

Even less can the Church accept that this evolution is moving in the direction of religious indifferentism, to the point that, in the future Christian world, the progress of the State would consist in the equality of all Christian religions.

If we read propositions 77 and 79 condemned by the *Syllabus*, we see that this is indeed the doctrine of the Church.[61]

these two powers. It denies the Catholic Church indirect power over mixed matters. It asserts that the State must be indifferent in religious matters concerning the faithful; that the same freedom must be granted to truth as to error; that the Church must not have privileges and favors or rights more extensive than those granted to other religious denominations, not even in Catholic countries [...]." (*Pontifical Documents of His Holiness Pius XII*, Year 1950, Vol. XII, Saint-Maurice, ed. de l'Œuvre de Saint-Augustin 1952, p. 75.)

60 In his speech at the Lateran University on March 2, 1953, His Eminence Cardinal Alfredo Ottaviani declared: "The Catholic Church insists on the principle that truth must prevail over error, and that the true religion, when it is known, must be helped in its spiritual mission in preference to religions whose message is more or less flawed, and where error is mixed with truth. This is a simple consequence of what man owes to truth. It would be very wrong, however, to conclude that this principle can only be applied by demanding for the true religion the favors of an absolutist power, or the assistance of dragonnades, or that the Catholic Church claims from modern societies the privileges it enjoyed in a sacral civilization, as in the Middle Ages."

61 Proposition (condemned) 77: "In the present day it is no longer expedient that the Catholic religion should be held as the only religion of the State, to the exclusion of all other forms of worship." (DS 2977); proposition (condemned) 79: "Moreover, it is false that the civil liberty

In this famous document, the immortal Pius IX condemns the opinion of those who think that equality of religions means progress (proposition 77, DS 2977), and of those who deny that such equality leads to religious indifference (proposition 79, DS 2979).

The words "Christendom," "Pharisaic," and "vital" deserve further comment.

Christendom is a temporal order of things based on the doctrine of Jesus Christ. If only the Catholic Church teaches this doctrine authentically, how can a "Christendom" build itself up while maintaining an equal distance from what the Church teaches and what heretical sects preach? Let us take a concrete example: if this "Christendom" allows divorce, will the organization of the family be Christian? And if it rejects divorce, can it claim to be inspired by "Christian" sects that favor divorce as much as by Catholic doctrine?

On the other hand, it seems that the word "Pharisaic" resonates as an insult to the Church. If the union of Church and State has always been the only regime accepted by the Church; if, despite the disorders that have existed here and there, it has been approved, maintained, and practiced by so many popes, by so many kings raised to the honors of the altar, how can we conceive that such a regime could be described as "pharisaical" without inferring the most insulting consequences for the Holy See and for so many saints?

As for "vital," what exactly does this expression mean? Vital normally means: having life. Was not the civilization that emerged from the hands of the Church in the Middle Ages "vitally" Christian? Is there any hope that the interdenominational state of the future "Christendom" will be "vitally" Christian?

To conclude these remarks, it is important to recall that

of every form of worship, and the full power, given to all, of overtly and publicly manifesting any opinions whatsoever and thoughts, conduce more easily to corrupt the morals and minds of the people, and to propagate the pest of indifferentism." (DS 2979).

the union between Church and·State necessarily implies the greatest independence of the Church from civil authority in all matters of spiritual or mixed power. Especially in modern times, this order has been distorted by the State's increasing interference in ecclesiastical matters. Such encroachments must be condemned outright, and the freedom of the Church must be asserted, but without renouncing the principle of her union with the State. And when, in a country, the evil is so deep that circumstances impose separation as a lesser evil, because union would necessarily be distorted, one must fear for that country. For nothing that separates itself from God and his Church can last very long. One of the worst effects of the separation of Church and State — even when it is a lesser evil — is the distortion that occurs in the popular mentality, which becomes accustomed to viewing temporal life in a totally naturalistic way. This creates deeply secularized minds, and we must recognize that, under such a system of relations, it is very difficult to shape the soul of an entire people in accordance with the right thinking that subordinates temporal life to the service of God.

– 67 –

The political duty of Catholics consists solely in promoting the temporal good. On behalf of the Church, they must limit themselves to asking the State for the freedoms granted to any private association.

Catholics must act in politics not only to promote the common good in the temporal sphere, but also to obtain recognition by the State of the Church as a public law society, sovereign in its sphere and endowed with all the prerogatives that belong to it as the only true Church.

Explanation

The refuted proposition is influenced by two errors: that of the "new morality," which, on this point, considers the temporal common good as an end in itself, entirely independent of any other sphere; and that which postulates equality between the true Church, on the one hand, and false "churches" and private associations, on the other.

Thus, the refuted maxim logically leads to the proposition condemned by Pius IX in the Syllabus, which declares lawful education separate from the Catholic faith and the authority of the Church, and oriented exclusively or principally toward the knowledge of natural realities and earthly social good (proposition 48, DS 2948).[62] It also leads to the error of proposition 54 of the same Syllabus, which holds that civil authority should be placed above ecclesiastical authority (DS 2954).[63]

– 68 –

In selecting immigrants, their beliefs are irrelevant: it is sufficient to consider the economic, ethnic, and political advantages.
In selecting immigrants, their beliefs must be taken into account first and foremost, and not just economic, ethnic, and political needs.

Explanation

The unity of a country in the true faith is its highest spiritual good. It is obvious that such unity can be broken if borders are opened to migratory flows that end up forming religious tumors as dangerous in the spiritual realm as social tumors are in the political realm. The refuted maxim, which reflects the Secularism of previous proposals, ignores these

---

62 Proposition (condemned) 48: "Catholics may approve of the system of educating youth unconnected with Catholic faith and the power of the Church, and which regards the knowledge of merely natural things, and only, or at least primarily, the ends of earthly social life."

63 Proposition (condemned) 54: "Kings and princes are not only exempt from the jurisdiction of the Church, but are superior to the Church in deciding questions of jurisdiction."

considerations.

Furthermore, it was expressly condemned by Pope Pius IX in proposition 78 of the Syllabus, which states: "Hence it has been wisely decided by law, in some Catholic countries, that persons coming to reside therein shall enjoy the public exercise of their own peculiar worship" (condemned proposition, DS 2978).

For, in matters of immigration, attention to the religious factor must come first. Although it is a natural right of overpopulated nations to be able to send emigrants to countries capable of receiving them, it is nevertheless necessary that, in the exercise of this right, fidelity to the Church, required by the superior right of Catholic populations, be recognized. In other words, when circumstances oblige Catholic countries to receive immigrants from pagan or heretical countries, a series of measures—complex in themselves, moreover—is necessary to ensure that such immigration does not take place to the spiritual detriment of Catholic populations.

See, in this regard, all the solicitude that the Holy See shows in providing spiritual assistance to immigrants in the apostolic constitution *Exsul Familia* of August 1, 1952 (AAS 44, page 649 and following).[64]

---

64 French text in *Documents pontificaux de S. S. Pie XII*, year 1952, vol. XIV, Saint-Maurice, ed. de l'Œuvre de Saint-Augustin, 1955, p. 337 ff. The first part of the constitution deals with what the Church has done specifically for Catholic emigrants; the second part gives "the rules for the spiritual assistance of emigrants" (see especially chap. IV: On the responsibility for souls to be exercised by the local Ordinaries in relation to foreigners," p. 395 ff.).

— 69 —

Catholics must unite, on social and economic grounds, with any group, current, or political movement that helps them against Capitalism. Thus, they can accept, in their relations with Communists, the so-called policy of the outstretched hand.

Catholics may agree to join forces with other movements, currents of thought, or groups if, by chance, they pursue the same immediate goal. However, this does not authorize ongoing collaboration with a group professing a different doctrine. With regard to Communists, since the ultimate goals, the means employed, and the spirit with which each one pursues their goal are different, there is a real impossibility of continued collaboration. Such collaboration could, moreover, seriously harm Catholics and lead the public into dangerous confusion. Catholics must always avoid, when intervening in social issues, appearing to support class struggle.

Explanation

The refuted sentence is fully in line with the principles of Secularism and religious indifference of the previous propositions. It subordinates all spiritual and doctrinal interests to the sole pursuit of occasional successes and favors the worst enemies of the Church.

Let us recall that Communists were the subject of a special condemnation by the Holy Office (July 1, 1949, AAS 41, page 334).[65]

65 Decree of the Holy Office against Communism of July 1, 1949 (DS 3865): " (1) Is it licit to join or show favor to Communist parties? (2) Is it licit to publish, distribute, or read publications that support Communist doctrine or activity, or to write for them? (3) May Christians who knowingly and freely commit the acts in parts 1 and 2 be given the sacraments? (4) Do Christians who profess, defend, or promote materialistic Communist doctrine incur the penalty of excommunication as apostates from the Christian faith, with the penalty reserved so that it may only be lifted by the Holy See?"

"Answer (confirmed by the Supreme Pontiff on June 30, 1949): For

VIII — On Political, Economic, and Social Issues

— 70 —

Jesus Christ preached poverty and humility, and gave preference to the weak and the lowly. A society imbued with this spirit must eliminate inequalities of wealth and social status. The political and social reforms that emerged from the French Revolution were, consciously or unconsciously, inspired by the Gospel and contributed to the creation of a truly Christian society.

1. Negative: Communism is indeed materialistic and Anti-Christian; although Communist leaders sometimes declare in words that they do not attack religion, they show in fact, either by doctrine or by action, that they are hostile to God, to true religion, and to the Church of Christ. For 2. Negative: they are in fact prohibited by law (see CIC [1917], can. 1399). For 3. Negative, in accordance with the ordinary principles concerning the refusal of the sacraments to those who do not have the required disposition. For 4. Affirmative."

> Jesus Christ preached the spirit of poverty and humility, and showed preference for the weak and the lowly. By poverty, the Church means detachment from earthly goods or the use of one's wealth in such a way that it serves the salvation of the soul and not its ruin. Thus, she has never taught that being rich is intrinsically evil, but only that it is evil to make disordered use of one's riches. By humility, the Church means this: that the faithful recognize that they possess nothing of their own but have received everything from God, and that they are content with their station in life. The existence of social classes is therefore a prerequisite for the practice of virtue and humility. As for the preference for the weak and the small, it would be impossible in a society where all were equal. The French Revolution, insofar as it sought complete political, social, and economic equality in the ideal society dreamed up by its authors, was a Satanic movement, inspired by pride.

Explanation

It is certain that inequalities, whether in the political, social, or economic sphere, have often been unjust, for two main reasons: either because these inequalities were illegitimate and resulted purely and simply from oppression; or because they were so pronounced that they denied man's natural dignity and deprived him of the means to live in good health and honesty.

A typical example of abusive inequality was the harsh and undeserved conditions in which the industrial revolution plunged workers in the 19th century (see Pius XI, *Quadragesimo anno*, AAS 23, pages 195, 197, and 198).[66] Contrary to what

---

66 For example: "Certainly, capital has long succeeded in arrogating excessive advantages to itself. It claimed for itself the totality of the product and the profit, leaving the working class barely enough to regain its strength and perpetuate itself. An inescapable economic law, it was claimed, dictated that all capital should accumulate in the hands of the rich; the same law condemned workers to lead the most precarious of existences in perpetual destitution..." (*Acts of His Holiness Pius XI*, vol. VI [1931], Bonne Presse, p. 120); "[...] The attenuation of poverty, which in the time of Leo XIII was still

has been said, the Church fulfilled its duty by opposing this situation. But in this struggle, its goal was to establish a hierarchical society within the limits set by the natural order. It never sought the abolition of all legitimate inequalities, as dreamed of by revolutionaries and pursued by Freemasonry and other subversive agents (see Pius XII, *Christmas radio message of 1944*, AAS, vol. 37, p. 14).[67]

– 71 –

The Church must make common cause with the worker in the struggle against the Capitalist system.
The Church intervenes in social issues to protect natural law. Its goal is not to favor one class over another, but to ensure that the doctrine of Jesus Christ prevails in relations between classes. It approves of the just aspirations of workers as well as the authentic rights of employers. The Capitalist system, insofar as it is based on private property, is legitimate in itself. The Church combats its abuses, but does not encourage its destruction.

Explanation

Among Catholics, the idea is spreading that the Church is a kind of labor party whose purpose is to defend a single class. On the contrary, the Church stands above classes as it stands above parties. Even when it defends the just demands of

---

widespread in all its horror..." (*Ibid.*, p. 123).

67 Radio message at Christmas 1944: "In a people worthy of the name, all inequalities that derive not from free caprice but from the very nature of things – inequalities of culture, wealth, social position, without prejudice, of course, to justice and mutual charity – are in no way an obstacle to the existence and predominance of a genuine spirit of community and fraternity. On the contrary, far from harming civil equality in any way, they give it its legitimate meaning, namely that everyone has the right, before the State, to live their own personal life honorably, in the position and conditions in which the designs and dispositions of Providence have placed them." (*Pontifical Documents of His Holiness Pius XII*, 1944, vol. VI, Saint-Maurice, ed. de l'Œuvre de Saint-Augustin, 1963, p. 246.)

workers, it never disregards the rights of employers. Not long ago, in an address to the *Katholikentag* in Vienna (September 14, 1952; see *Catolicismo* No. 24, December 1952), the Pope clearly stated that the labor issue, which was a burning issue in the first half of the 20th century, had now been superseded by another more serious issue, that of the class struggle inspired by Socialism.[68] It is more necessary than ever to show that the Church is the protector of all, workers and employers alike, and not just the systematic advocate of one against the other.

As for Capitalism, we must dispel the confusion that common language perpetuates about it. The Capitalist system, in itself, that is, as a system based on private property and free enterprise, allowing profits to the extent permitted by morality, is legitimate and cannot be confused with the abuses to which it has given rise in many places.

It is therefore important to distinguish between the legitimate defense of healthy workers' organizations against the abuses of Capitalism and the struggle of revolutionary organizations that proclaim the illegitimacy of the Capitalist system itself. Anyone who associates themselves with the actions of the latter is collaborating with Communism and incurs the blame contained in the letter from the Sacred Congregation of Seminaries to the Brazilian episcopate: "For some, the guidelines promulgated by the Holy See, mainly

68 Radio message to *the Katholikentag* in Vienna, September 14, 1952: "[...] Today, the Church recalls the first period of contemporary social struggles. At the center was the labor question: the misery of the proletariat and the duty to raise this class of men, defenseless against the vagaries of the economic situation, to the dignity of the other classes of society endowed with specific rights. This problem can now be considered solved, at least in its essential parts, and the Catholic world has contributed to this solution in a loyal and effective manner. [...] If the signs of the times are not misleading, other problems dominate in the second era of social struggles, which we seem to have entered. We will name two of these problems: overcoming class struggle and defending the individual and the family. Class struggle must be overcome by establishing an organic order that unites employers and workers. The class struggle can never be an objective of Catholic social doctrine. The Church is always indebted to all classes of society." (*Pontifical Documents of His Holiness Pius XII*, 1952, vol. XIV, p. 469.)

from Leo XIII to Pius XII, which are so humane and so wisely favorable to the working classes, are not sufficient in the social sphere, but they strive to move ever closer to the left, to the point of entertaining a real sympathy for Bolshevik Communism, which destroys religion and all that is truly good for the human person" (AAS 42, page 841).

— 72 —

The wage system is contrary to human dignity and intrinsically unjust. The condition of being a worker naturally entails the right to participate in the ownership of the enterprise, its management, and its profits.
The wage system is entirely consistent with human and Christian dignity. An employment contract does not necessarily imply that the worker has a share in the ownership, management, or profits of the enterprise.

Explanation

Leo XIII, St. Pius X, Pius XI (see *Quadragesimo anno*, AAS 23, page 199)[69], and Pius XII teach that the wage system is, in itself, just and in accordance with human dignity. The unhealthy economy of the 19th and 20th centuries has stripped the wage system of its true character. According to Church doctrine, relations between employers and workers are marked by a family character. Employees were once considered full members of the domestic society, which included spouses, family, and the entire community subject to the head of the house. The word "boss" [*patrão*], which comes from *pater*, father, and the word "domestic" [*criado*], which derives

---

69 "Let us begin by pointing out the profound error of those who declare the contract of employment to be fundamentally unjust and claim that it must be replaced by a partnership contract; in saying this, they are in fact seriously insulting our Predecessor [Leo XIII], for the encyclical *Rerum novarum* not only admits the legitimacy of wage labor, but also devotes considerable space to regulating it according to standards of justice. (*Quadragesimo anno, Acts of His Holiness Pius XI*, vol. VII [1931], Bonne Presse, p. 126).

from the fact that servants were trained and educated in the father's own house [*casa* in Portuguese, *domus* in Latin], are reminders of this character. This is enough to show that there is nothing derogatory about being a salaried employee. Even in the industrial and commercial world, the family character of these relationships must continue to exist. The Church wants employers and workers to be with each other, as far as possible, like members of the same family, father and son, working together for the common good.

From the point of view of justice, wages are a satisfactory system of remuneration, provided that they meet the conditions laid down by Pius XI, that is, if they are sufficient to ensure an honest and dignified livelihood for the worker and his family. This honest and dignified livelihood includes the necessary comfort that will enable the provident worker to build up savings and improve the situation of his own family. In this way, he also participates in the increase in prosperity that technical and productive progress brings to society (see *Quadragesimo Anno*: "The resources that are constantly being accumulated by the progress of the social economy must therefore be distributed among individuals and the various classes of society in such a way as to provide the common good referred to by Leo XIII, or, to express the same idea in other words, to respect the common good of society as a whole" (AAS 23, page 196).[70]

Pius XI and Pius XII present the participation of workers in the profits of the enterprise as a commendable practice, but never as an obligation (see Radio message to the *Katholikentag* already cited).[71] In some cases, it can produce good results.

70 *Quadragesimo anno*, *Acts of His Holiness Pius XI*, vol. VII [1931], Bonne Presse, p. 122.
71 Radio message to the *Katholikentag*, September 14, 1952: "This explains the insistence of Catholic social doctrine, particularly on the right to private property. This is the profound reason why the popes of the social encyclicals and We ourselves have refused to deduce, either directly or indirectly, from the nature of the employment contract, the worker's right to co-ownership of capital and, consequently, his right to co-management. [...]" (*Pontifical Documents of His Holiness Pius XII*, Year 1952, Vol. XIV, Saint-Maurice, ed.

But it is not a panacea that must always be applied. Above all, it cannot be imposed by law on an entire country. The same must be said of worker participation in the ownership or management of the company. On this last point, Catholic doctrine only allows such participation on condition that the decision-making power and responsibility for the running of the factory or commercial establishment remain in the hands of the owner of the enterprise (see Pius XII, *Address to the 9th Congress of the International Union of Catholic Employers' Associations*, AAS 41, page 285).[72]

The refuted statement, taken to its extreme conclusion, would mean the abolition of class inequality, the ultimate goal dreamed of by all revolutionaries.

— 73 —

According to St. Augustine, the sole owner of all wealth is God. Man is only its manager. Wealth therefore belongs to the community, and the owner is merely its administrator, subordinate to the common good.

---

de l'Œuvre de Saint-Augustin, 1955, p. 469.) See also DS 3733 (*Quadragesimo anno.*)

72 Address to the members of the International Union of Catholic Employers' Associations, May 7, 1949: "Nor would it be true to assert that every private enterprise is by its nature a society, so that the relations between its participants are determined by the rules of distributive justice, in such a way that all, without distinction — whether or not they are owners of the means of production — would be entitled to their share of the property or at least of the profits of the enterprise. Such a conception starts from the assumption that every enterprise by its nature falls within the sphere of public law. [...] The owner of the means of production, whoever he may be — private owner, workers' association, or foundation — must, always within the limits of public economic law, remain master of his economic decisions. It goes without saying that his income is higher than that of his collaborators. [...]" (Pontifical Documents of His Holiness Pius XII, 1949, vol. XI, pp. 161-162.)

According to St. Augustine, the supreme owner of all wealth is God. It follows that the owner must use his property according to God's sovereign will. However, God is not identified with the community. While God's empire over all wealth is absolute, that of the community is not. Transferring God's rights to a community is tantamount to deifying the State and sacrificing the individual.

Explanation

The refuted proposition is "statolatric." That is why it reaches conclusions that are only admissible in a conception that makes the state a god. In reality, the system of individual property ownership stems from the idea that the state is neither a god nor an end in itself, but rather a means. Therefore, the status of owner means the exercise of a personal and individual right, not the exercise of a right delegated by the state. And that is why we say that the owner cannot in any way be confused with a mere manager.

What characterizes a manager, in fact, is the exercise of rights that are not his own, but have been delegated to him. And that is why the distinction between owner and manager is common in the laws of non-Communist countries (see *Quadragesimo anno*, AAS 23).[73]

---

73 "What strikes us most in our time is not only the concentration of wealth, but also the accumulation of enormous power, of discretionary economic power, in the hands of a small number of men who are usually not the owners, but merely the custodians and managers of the capital they administer at will. This power is especially considerable in those who, as absolute holders and masters of money, govern credit and dispense it according to their pleasure. In this way, they distribute, as it were, the lifeblood to the economic organism whose life they hold in their hands, so that without their consent, no one can breathe." (*Quadragesimo anno, Acts of His Holiness Pius XI*, vol. VII [1931], Bonne Presse, pp. 146-147).

— 74 —

The only title to property, in the strict sense of the term, is labor, so that man is only the owner of what he personally produces. The natural resources he possesses do not belong to him absolutely; he is only their administrator and possesses them only to the extent that he administers them, since their absolute ownership belongs to the community.

Leo XIII teaches that the original title to property is not labor, but occupation. Thus, man is the owner not only of the fruits of his labor, but also of natural resources, that is, not only of the fruits of the earth, but also of the earth itself. And he may exploit it himself or through others.

Explanation

The refuted proposition is identical with what is called "Agrarian Socialism," which denies land ownership. This opinion is condemned by Catholic sociologists who rely on the argument by which Leo XIII, in *Rerum Novarum*, justifies private property.[74] And, in fact, in this encyclical, the Pope shows that man also has a right to legitimately acquired property. See also the doctrine of *Quadragesimo Anno*, reproduced in the explanation of number 71. In the same encyclical, Pius XI explicitly rejects the opinion of those who consider labor to be the sole title to property.[75]

---

74 "You are not unaware, venerable brothers and dear sons, of the energy with which our predecessor [Leo XIII], of happy memory, defended private property against the Socialist errors of his time and how he showed that its abolition, far from serving the interests of the working class, could only seriously compromise them. " (*Quadragesimo anno*, ibid., pp. 112-113.)

75 "Universal tradition, no less than the teachings of our predecessor [Leo XIII], make the occupation of ownerless property and the work that transforms a material (*occupatione rei nullius et industria seu specificatione*) the original titles of property. In fact, contrary to certain opinions, there is no injustice in occupying vacant property that belongs to no one. On the other hand, the work that man performs in his own name and by which he gives an object a new form or increases its value is the only thing that gives him a right to the product." (*Quadragesimo anno*, ibid., p. 118; DS 3730.)

— 75 —

The land itself cannot be appropriated by individuals, as it belongs to the community. Therefore, those who live off the land must pay the community for the benefits they derive from its exclusive use. The state can collect this fee through a tax system that levies all taxes on the land. And since the land is the natural source of all goods, such a tax should be sufficient to provide for all the needs of the State.

Land, like any other movable or immovable property, is subject to individual appropriation. Therefore, the owner of the land owes the state no special contribution for its exclusive exploitation. Taxes must fall on owners as much as on any other person, according to the rules of distributive justice. Land is not the sole source of economic goods. A tax levied exclusively on land would subvert the private economy and would be insufficient to support the normal expenses of the state.

Explanation

The refuted statement is one of the classic theses of Henry George's "Agrarian Socialism." The Church is far from sharing this phobia of land ownership. On the contrary, it sees in this ownership a valuable support for the stability of families, social classes, pious and charitable associations, and ecclesiastical institutions.

— 76 —

Large estates are intrinsically evil because they are contrary to Christian doctrine, which only accepts small properties, more in line with the equality that should reign among men.

It is desirable that property be distributed as widely as possible among men, because it is the natural prerogative of the individual. Social prosperity, however, implies and sometimes requires that, alongside small property, there also be medium and large properties. Equality among men must be understood not in the sense of leveling, but in the sense of proportion: rights and responsibilities correspond to the position that the person occupies in society.

Explanation

Since property also fulfills a social function, there are necessarily limits to large property, namely: when, to the detriment of the common good, it promotes the unproductivity of wealth; when it concentrates wealth in the hands of a few to the point of reducing others to misery, destitution, or servitude; when it prevents a significant portion of men from becoming property owners. (See the explanation of proposition 71.)

Pope Pius XII spoke on the legitimacy of large estates in his address of July 2, 1951, to the members of the Congress meeting in Rome to study the improvement of the living conditions of agricultural workers (AAS 43, page 554 ff.). After discussing the appropriateness of small rural property ["We are thinking here primarily of peasant farms, family farms: this is the rural class which, by its social character as a whole, and also by its economic role, forms the nucleus of a healthy peasantry"], the Pope added: "This does not mean denying the usefulness, and often the necessity, of larger agricultural holdings."[76]

— 77 —

The social question is a question of pure justice in economic matters. To resolve it, we must not resort to charity.

---

76 *Address to the Third International Catholic Rural Congress*, July 2, 1951. *Pontifical Documents of His Holiness Pius XII*, Year 1951, vol. XIII, Saint-Maurice, ed. de l'Œuvre de Saint-Augustin, 1954, p. 288.

> The social question is above all a moral and religious question (Leo XIII, *Graves de communi*). It encompasses questions of justice and charity, and will never be resolved by the exercise of the duties of justice alone.

Explanation

The refuted proposition is in harmony with Historical Materialism, which does not take into account the human soul in the social question, but only the body and its needs. The Church teaches that the social question is above all a moral one; and, since all moral questions are religious, it is therefore essentially religious.

Leo XIII, in *Rerum novarum*, teaches that the social question can only be solved if two principles are accepted: 1) social inequality; 2) the necessity of the union of social classes. In developing this second principle, he indicates the means that must be employed to achieve this union, namely:

1. justice;

2. friendship, which leads the rich not only to fulfill their duties of strict justice, but also to be generous in giving of their surplus. He adds that this duty of almsgiving is a true moral obligation and that Providence has arranged it this way to promote unity between the classes.[77] It was the design of Providence, in giving some more than others, either in terms of talents or wealth, that some should serve others by distributing their surplus and that all should thus live united and as friends;

3. thirdly, the sentiment of Christian charity, which, by entering into the various relationships established between classes, imbues social life with that well-ordered sweetness which is the perfection of human community life.

---

77 See also DS 3729 (*Quadragesimo anno*): "The rich are bound by a very serious precept to practice almsgiving, charity, and generosity, as taught by the Holy Scriptures and the Holy Fathers of the Church."

Leo XIII is therefore far from restricting the social question to the narrow and petty limits of *"do ut facias"* [I give so that you may do]. He approaches the question in a humane manner, considering that Our Lord God created all creatures for the same ultimate purpose, which must be achieved through the multifaceted assistance that each person gives to others here on earth.

In *Graves de communi*, written ten years later, in 1901, Leo XIII categorically states that the social question will not be solved by wage increases, reduced working hours, or other measures of this kind; social peace is the fruit of virtue, which only religion can firmly implant.

The same doctrine is taught by Pius XI in *Quadragesimo anno*, which points out that the cause of society's ills lies in economic development that has taken place on the margins of moral principles and even contrary to those principles.[78]

– 78 –

The Church was wrong in the past when it approved monarchical and aristocratic regimes that promote inequality and class pride and are therefore incompatible with the spirit of the Gospel.

---

78 See the last part of the encyclical (*Acts of His Holiness Pius XI*, ibid., p. 160 ff.).

> In itself, the Church considers that the three systems—monarchical, aristocratic, and democratic—are equally compatible with its principles and therefore with the spirit of the Gospel. St. Thomas teaches that, in principle, the best regime is the monarchical regime, but, given human contingencies, the best system of government must include elements of each of these three regimes (I-II, q. 105, a. 1, *corpus et ad* 1 83).[79]

Explanation

The refuted sentence was condemned by Saint Pius X in the apostolic letter *Notre Charge Apostolique* against the *Sillon*, a Modernist propaganda organ directed by Marc Sangnier. In this document, the saintly pope declares that Christian civilization, according to Leo XIII, is possible in any of the three forms of government.[80]

---

79 "[...] Here, then, is the best organization for the government of a city or kingdom: at the head is placed, on account of his virtue, a single leader with authority over all; then come a number of subordinate leaders, qualified by their virtue; and yet the multitude is not alien to the power thus defined, all having the possibility of being elected and all being, on the other hand, electors. Such is the perfect regime, happily mixed with monarchy through the preeminence of one, aristocracy through the multiplicity of virtuously qualified leaders, and finally democracy or popular power through the fact that ordinary citizens can be chosen as leaders and that the choice of leaders belongs to the people. And such was the regime instituted by divine law. Indeed, Moses and his successors governed the people as sole and universal leaders, which is a characteristic of kingship. But the seventy-two elders were elected on the basis of their merit (Deut. 1:15): 'I took wise and respected men from your tribes and appointed them as leaders;' this is the element of aristocracy. As for democracy, it was affirmed in that the leaders were taken from among the people as a whole (Ex. 18:21): 'Choose capable men from among all the people,' etc.; and that the people also appointed them (Deut. 1:13): 'Present wise men from among you.' The excellence of the legal provisions is therefore indisputable with regard to the organization of powers." (*Summa Theologica*, vol. 2, Paris, Cerf, 1984, p. 702.)

80 "Thus [for the *Sillon*], democracy alone will usher in the reign of perfect justice! Is this not an insult to other forms of government, which are thus relegated to the rank of impotent stopgap governments? Moreover, Le *Sillon* still clashes with the teaching of Leo XIII on this point. He could have read in the aforementioned encyclical on political principles [*Diuturnum*

Furthermore, the refuted maxim comes from the false assumption that [social] equality among men was taught by Jesus Christ. All pontifical documents relating to social issues establish, as a foundation willed by Providence, the inequality of classes. Thus, for example: *Rerum novarum*, *Quadragesimo anno*, the Christmas Radio Message of 1944, etc.

— 79 —

Christian democracy consists in the government of the people, that is, of the majority.

"Christian democracy" is an expression used to indicate any government that promotes the common good in obedience to God's law, whether that government is monarchical, aristocratic, or democratic. This is what Leo XIII teaches when he says that Christian democracy "must not in any way have in view the preference or preparation of one form of government over another" (*Graves de communi*). The democratic form of government is compatible with the doctrine of the Church insofar as it means the participation of the people in public affairs. However, by "people," the Church does not mean the numerical, inorganic majority, that is, the masses, but rather the entire population, taking into account legitimate differences in class, region, etc. Legitimate democracy is therefore not the domination of the most numerous classes over the least numerous, of the masses over the elite, but the just and proportionate influence of classes, families, regions, and social groups in public affairs.

Explanation

illud] that 'justice being safeguarded, it is not forbidden for peoples to give themselves the government that best suits their character or the institutions and customs they have received from their ancestors;' and the encyclical alludes to the well-known three forms of government. It therefore assumes that justice is compatible with each of them." (*Pontifical Documents of His Holiness Saint Pius X*, vol. II, 1909-1914, publications of the Courrier de Rome, 1993, p. 257.)

The difference between the Catholic concept and the common concept of democracy stems from the way the word "people" is understood.

For the Church, the people are, in a certain sense, the opposite of the "masses." Pius XII says:

"The people and the amorphous multitude (or, as it is commonly called, the masses) are two different concepts. The people live and move by its own life; the masses are inert in themselves and can only be moved from outside. The people lives from the fullness of the lives of the individuals who compose it, each of whom, in his own place and in his own way, is a person conscious of his own responsibilities and convictions. The masses, on the contrary, await impetus from outside, easily manipulated by anyone who exploits their instincts and impressions, quick to follow, today one flag and tomorrow another. The vital exuberance of a true people spreads life, abundant and rich, throughout the State and all its organs, infusing them with a constantly renewed vigor, an awareness of their own responsibilities, and a true sense of the common good." [Christmas radio message, 1944.][81]

Now, for ordinary democrats, the people is precisely what Pius XII calls the masses. This is what emerges from his words:

"[In the national and constitutional sphere.] Everywhere today, the life of nations is being disrupted by the blind worship of numerical value. The citizen is a voter. But as such, he is in reality only one of the units that make up a majority or a minority, which a shift of a few votes, even a single vote, is enough to reverse. In the eyes of the parties, they count only for their electoral value, for the support their vote brings; their place and role as heads of families and in their professions are not taken into account." [Address to the leaders of the Universal Movement for a World Confederation, April 6, 1951.][82]

---

81 *Pontifical Documents of His Holiness Pius XII*, year 1944, vol. VI, Saint-Maurice, ed. de l'Œuvre de Saint-Augustin, 1963, p. 246.
82 *Pontifical Documents of His Holiness Pius XII*, Year 1951, vol. XIII, p. 119.

On the subject of democracy, it should be added that it can never, in the acceptable sense of the word, be identified with the revolutionary myth of popular sovereignty. All power comes from God at most; the people—and by "people" we mean what has been defined above, as opposed to the masses—can choose those who will govern them with the authority they have received from God.

— 80 —

| Catholics must prefer Socialism to Liberalism. |
| **Catholics must accept neither Liberalism nor Socialism.** |

Explanation

According to Church doctrine, both Liberal and Socialist regimes are bad; and when taken to their ultimate consequences, they produce the complete subversion of social life.

Catholics must therefore seek to establish a system that is based on a different foundation. The rejected proposal is wrong to view Liberalism and Socialism as if they were opposed to each other. In reality, as Leo XIII affirms, Liberalism is the cause of Socialism, because, given the secular and disorganized nature of our times, it is impossible to escape from one extreme without falling into the other. Take, for example, a society given over to Paganism: if the authorities are Liberal and condescending, if the laws allow individuals great freedom of movement, the frightening unleashing of passions inevitably leads to anarchy. Maintaining order then requires such a multiplicity of laws, decrees, and regulations, such a large number of public interventions to ensure the functioning of the countless functions of the state, that the isolated, defenseless, terrorized citizen quickly becomes a speck of dust, an inert slave in the face of the Moloch State. The foundations of the true solution, opposed to Liberalism and Socialism, can be found in the following words of the

Supreme Pontiff: "The state does not contain within itself, nor does it mechanically bring together in a given territory, an amorphous conglomerate of individuals; it is and must be, in reality, the principle of organic and organizing unity of a true people" (Christmas Message, 1948).[83]

---

83 We did not find this text in the Christmas radio message of 1948, which only says: "Catholic doctrine on the state and civil society has always been based on the principle that, according to divine will, peoples form together a community with a common purpose and common duties." Pontifical Documents of His Holiness Pius XII, Year 1948, vol. X, p. 450.

Directives

[Guidelines addressed to the clergy of the diocese]

1. In order to make your efforts to combat these errors more effective, we recommend that you use language of the utmost precision. In contemporary religious writings, most often intended for dissemination among the faithful, we read certain words that would be more appropriately found in strictly technical works addressed to specialists. However, these terms, as is natural, pass from writings to preaching and are used in conferences and meetings of religious associations, so that they become commonplace in certain circles. While some of these terms are excellent, others need to be given a precise meaning, and still others are simply unintelligible. All this results in considerable confusion among the general public, among whom these terms are widespread. Let us mention a few: pneumatic Church, living in the pneuma, transpsychological spirituality, religious anthropocentrism, Christocentric spirituality, living in a state of extreme tension, virtue-centrism, moralism, etc.

2. With regard to Holy Mass, it is important to always emphasize that the consecration is its essential and most important part; that the Mass, as a true sacrifice of the New Law, has four ends: latreutic, eucharistic, propitiatory, and impetrative; and that Communion is the excellent means of participating in the Holy Sacrifice, so as to exclude the idea that attendance at Mass alone is more important than sacramental Communion.

3. When expounding the doctrine of the Mystical Body, it is advisable to avoid any expression that might lead to a Pantheistic conception.

4. In instilling devotion to the Eternal Father, you must not speak of Jesus Christ as if he were merely a mediator. Such an approach would lead the faithful to think that

the second Person of the Most Holy Trinity cannot be the object of our adoration, but is merely an intermediary between us and God, our Lord. Special care must be taken in this regard in regions where spiritualism is spreading intensely, which, as you know, dear colleagues, denies the divinity of Jesus Christ.

5. Let us remember that, according to *Mediator Dei*, "to repudiate and reject polyphonic or polyphonic songs, even when they conform to the norms given by the Apostolic See," is outside "the right path" (AAS 39, pages 545-546).[84] The same encyclical recommends popular religious singing (ibid., page 590).[85]

6. On the use of Latin in the sacred liturgy, dear colleagues, pay attention to what Pope Pius XII wisely says in the same encyclical *Mediator Dei*: "The use of the Latin language, in use in a large part of the Church, is a manifest and striking sign of unity, and an effective protection against any corruption of the original doctrine" (AAS 39, page 545).[86]

7. Never miss an opportunity to teach true devotion to the Holy Father, the Pope, and, to a lesser degree, to the diocesan bishop. On this point, it is necessary to avoid a certain tendency which, with the laudable aim of strengthening the bonds of charity between the sheep and the local pastor, presents the bishop in such a light as to confer on him a kind of infallibility, almost making him equal to the Holy Father, who, according to this

84 *Pontifical Documents of His Holiness Pius XII*, year 1947, vol. IX, Saint-Maurice, ed. de l'Œuvre de Saint-Augustin, 1961, p. 375.
85 "However, modern music and singing cannot be completely excluded from Catholic worship, [...] provided that they are not profane or inappropriate... We urge you once again, venerable brothers, to take care to promote popular religious singing and its perfect execution" (ibid., pp. 417-418). The same encyclical, however, calls for the preservation and cultivation of Gregorian chant, "which the Church absolutely prescribes in certain parts of the liturgy [see St. Pius X, Apostolic Letter *Tra le sollecitudini*]."
86 *Pontifical Documents of His Holiness Pius XII*, year 1947, vol. IX, Saint-Maurice, éd. de l'Œuvre de Saint-Augustin, 1961, p. 374.

conception, would be merely a censor of the bishops. Therefore, teach the correct doctrine concerning the relationship between the pope and the bishops. Our Lord Jesus Christ instituted in the Church a single hierarchy of government, consisting of two degrees that are in harmony: the pope and, subordinate to him, the bishops (CIC, can. 108, § 3).[87] The unity of this hierarchy is an indispensable concept for the faithful to know how to position themselves in relation to it. By seeing it as a single whole, with the Supreme Pontiff at its summit, the source of all jurisdiction in the Church, and by considering the bishops and the Pope in the same perspective, the faithful will show them all the respect, veneration, and love they owe them. In this regard, it should be remembered that fullness of power belongs to the Roman Pontiff, who has direct and immediate jurisdiction over the bishops and all the faithful. The jurisdiction of the bishops, successors of the apostles, is exercised in harmony with and under the authority of the papal jurisdiction. Such is the natural framework of the Church. To seek to instill a devotion to the pope that is entirely different from and even opposed to devotion to the bishop, and vice versa, to seek to instill a devotion to the bishop that is different from and even opposed to devotion to the pope, would be to implicitly deny the harmonious unity of the hierarchy. Let us love the pope and the bishop with extreme charity and devotion, each according to his rank and in proportion to the powers conferred on them by Our Lord Jesus Christ. The most devoted faithful to his bishop — and every Catholic must be so — will have no fear of showing great respect for the supreme authority of the Roman Pontiff in all the extent conferred on him by the divine founder of the Church.

---

87 "By divine institution, the sacred hierarchy in respect of orders consists of Bishops, priests, and ministers; by reason of jurisdiction, [it consists of] the supreme pontificate and the subordinate episcopate; by institution of the Church other grades can also be added."

8. On the ecclesiastical magisterium, teach that since the papal magisterium is infallible and that of each bishop is official but fallible, it is in the order of human frailty that one bishop or another may fall into error. History records such occurrences. They produce, as one might expect, the most dangerous consequences. Nevertheless, it is necessary to teach the faithful how they should act in such circumstances. In such painful cases, the first duty of the faithful is to maintain all due respect for the sacred person of the pastor given to them by Providence and to faithfully carry out his orders in everything that does not hinder the direct and higher fidelity they owe to the Vicar of Christ.

9. Also instill veneration for ecclesiastical celibacy, which is one of the most legitimate glories of Catholic thought and of the Latin Church.

10. In dealing with the relationship between theology and philosophy, never adopt language that explicitly or implicitly denies the principle that philosophy is an auxiliary of theology. Show that true wisdom is found in Revelation, God's merciful gift to enlighten souls and lead them to salvation. Do not miss the opportunity to instill admiration for scholastic philosophy, and avoid showing indifference toward it by placing it on the same level as other philosophies. Likewise, do not allow it to be presented as outdated by new currents of modern thought or new apologetic schools.

11. Let the language of Catholics be entirely supernatural. Let us not be afraid to affirm at all times that we believe in Revelation, grace, and the divinity of the Church. Faith is God's greatest gift. It strengthens us in the knowledge most necessary to elevate our nature and guide our steps on the path that leads us to our eternal destiny. It would be lamentable if, in order not to displease the world, we showed any fear in affirming our faith. We would give the impression that it is not solid and that,

in our eyes, all religions are equal.

12. Similarly, let us reject an apologetic system that claims to appeal solely to the arguments of reason and is content to lead souls toward a purely natural religion, in the hope that the irremediable shortcomings of natural religion will prompt souls to find Revelation on their own.

13. An equal caution in language is recommended for everything related to social issues. We must not appear to be soldiers of any cause other than our own, nor give the impression of unilateral action incompatible with the sanctity of our mission. Above all, let us not flatter the great power of the day, which is the multitude, by suggesting that we are associated with the revolutionary progress that is now, through Communism, reaching the final stage of the destruction of the Western world. We hear it said everywhere that the Church is revolutionary and that if it does not fully reveal its positions, it is because it still needs the rich to build churches. It is easy to see the Opportunism, degrading Naturalism, and profound doctrinal corruption in this assertion. It is not in the service of "Mammon" that the Church fights against demagoguery and Socialism. But it is even less the slave of the multitude. We are the Mystical Body of Christ, which is immeasurably above all this and which struggles to establish on earth the reign of justice and charity without partiality.

14. Even greater caution is recommended in the formation of purity and in the explanation of conjugal duties. Catholic morality, like all the practices traditionally followed in the Church, perfectly guarantees, in the way it deals with these delicate subjects, all the decency of virtue. In an atmosphere of growing corruption, we must attach ourselves with redoubled fervor to our principles and traditions. We must avoid not only what is harmful to our moral perfection, but also any

attitude that could signify our approval of the sensual atmosphere of the modern world. Purity, in order to be fully and sustainably practiced, requires an atmosphere of dignity, gravity, and restraint. It is futile to imagine that this virtue can exist in groups where not only sin, but anything that could be described as the breath of evil, is not carefully avoided. Therefore, the faithful should not allow in their midst frivolous and more or less ambiguous expressions, carnival songs, or slang terms whose excessive triviality is not in harmony with the dignity that should reign in Catholic circles.

15. In studying issues related to the Church's current activities, may our dear colleagues be realistic without, however, compromising with the spirit of novelty, which attacks everything old for the sake of being old, tends to praise everything new for the sole fact of being new, and thus separates itself from the true traditional spirit of the Holy Church, as shown in the letter from the Sacred Congregation of Seminaries to the Brazilian episcopate: "The spirit of novelty will never cease to criticize anything that, even with obvious advantages, has been practiced until today. Any abuse or exaggeration in traditional customs and methods of apostolate is used to ridicule and treat everything as a whole with hostility" (AAS 42, page 840).[88]

Dear sons and beloved colleagues, it is very important for priests to teach. But what is teaching worth if it is not accompanied by love? Woe to knowledge, Bossuet exclaimed, that does not transform itself into love and action!

Knowing God and His Holy Church is a normal condition for salvation. But it is not enough to know God, we must worship Him; it is not enough to know the doctrine of the

---

88 Letter from the Sacred Congregation of Seminaries to the episcopate of Brazil (March 7, 1950); *Pontifical Documents of His Holiness Pius XII*, year 1950, vol. XII, Saint-Maurice, éd. de l'Œuvre de Saint-Augustin, 1952, p. 74.

Holy Church, we must love it with an enthusiastic and extreme love, a clear and ardent reflection of the love we owe to God.

When explaining to your parishioners the errors we have pointed out, explain to them, above all, the truths that oppose these errors. Form them in such a way that they do not stop at knowledge, but also attain love. In other words, instill in their souls that ardent love of orthodoxy, that attachment to the Catholic cause, of which you, as priests, are naturally living and edifying examples.

You must ask for this virtue of Catholic sensibility for your parishioners, as we ourselves ask for it for ourselves and for all our diocesans, in an unworthy but incessant prayer. Teach them also to ask for it for themselves. And so that our prayers, yours, beloved sons and dear co-workers, and those of all our dear diocesans, may be accepted by God, as we conclude this letter, let us humbly turn our gaze to the Sacred Heart of Jesus, the abyss of all virtues, the furnace of charity, the center and model of all hearts. May the lukewarmness of our souls be transformed into ardent zeal through contact with the flames that spring from the divine Heart. May our faults, our miseries, our unworthiness, draw upon us the mercy of this divine Heart, which is an abyss of charity. May the graces that flow from this divine Heart pour out upon us in all their fullness, to enlighten our minds and strengthen our wills, so that we may attain, to the extent that has been destined for us, that holiness which is the supreme desire of our souls.

In order for this to happen and for us to receive the full outpouring of graces from the Heart of Jesus, let us draw close to the Immaculate Heart of Mary, the necessary channel through which our prayers go to the Heart of Jesus and through which graces descend from the divine Heart to us. The Immaculate Heart of Mary has appeared in our day to the shepherd children of Fatima to ask us to do penance and to promise us the most special graces. Let us listen to the call of this maternal Heart and, trusting in her intercession, let us work, dear sons and beloved co-workers, so that the reign of the Sacred Heart may be established as soon as possible in our diocese. With our eyes fixed on this ideal, we give to all of you and to our beloved sons, your parishioners, with paternal affection, our pastoral blessing.

In the name of the Father, and of the Son, and of the Holy Ghost. Amen.

Given and transmitted in our episcopal city of Campos, under seal and the sign of our arms, on January 6, 1953, on the feast of the Epiphany of Our Lord Jesus Christ.

† Antonio, Bishop of Campos.

Mandatum

In the name of the Lord, we request and determine the following:

1. that the subject of our Pastoral Letter be explained to the faithful during Sunday Mass;

2. that the Catechism and its Guidelines, which form part of our Pastoral Letter, be explained, section by section, at meetings of religious and apostolic associations, for the Catholic formation of the members of these associations;

3. that the receipt and subject matter of this Pastoral Letter be recorded in the *Tombo* book [archive register] and that a copy be kept in the parish archives.

Given and transmitted in our episcopal city of Campos, under the seal and sign of our arms, on January 6, 1953, on the feast of the Epiphany of Our Lord Jesus Christ.

† Antonio, Bishop of Campos.

Discover Our Other Books:

The 1955 Holy Week, Fr. Olivier Rioult — $10 (ebook), $13 (paperback)

The Una Cum Issue and the Honor of God, Fr. Francesco Ricossa — $10 (ebook) to $13 (paperback)

Modernism in the Church, Charles Périn — $10 (ebook), $13 (paperback)

Christ in the Home, Fr. Raoul Plus — $19 (paperback)

The Four Temperaments, Rev. Conrad Hock — $7 (paperback)

The Anti-Christian Conspiracy, Msgr. Henri Delassus —$25 per part (pre-release translation project)

Life of Blessed Noël Pinot, Msgr. Alexis Crosnier —$16 (ebook), $24 (paperback)